the
internet
for students

Chris Wright

TEACH YOURSELF BOOKS

Orders: please contact Bookpoint Ltd, 39 Milton Park, Abingdon, Oxon OX14 4TD. Telephone: (44) 01235 400414, Fax: (44) 01235 400454. Lines are open 9.00 – 6.00, Monday to Saturday, with a 24 hour message answering service. E-mail address: orders@bookpoint.co.uk

A catalogue record for this title is available from the British Library.

ISBN 0 340 73032 3

First published 1999
Impression number   10 9 8 7 6 5 4 3 2 1
Year   2004 2003 2002 2001 2000 1999

Typeset by MacDesign, Southampton
Printed in Great Britain for Hodder & Stoughton Educational, a division of Hodder Headline Plc, 338 Euston Road, London NW1 3BH by Cox & Wyman, Reading, Berkshire.

CONTENTS

ACKNOWLEDGEMENTS

Of the many products referred to in this book, those that are registered trademarks are acknowledged as being the property of their owners. The AltaVista logo and search engine content are copyright and trademarks of Compaq Corporation. Used with permission.

I would like to thank all those people and organizations who have given permission for their Web sites or products to be portrayed and whose interest in this project has been a major source of motivation on days when the temperature moved into the high seventies and the tennis court seemed like a more attractive place to be!

Thanks are also due to Brenda McWalters for her unflagging support throughout this project and to the students, past and present, of the School of Informatics and Multimedia Technology at the University of North London.

INTRODUCTION

An Internet book specifically for students? Why?

Students represent a distinct user group; they enjoy free, unlimited access to the Internet and are responsible for much of the Web innovation. Netscape itself has origins in a student project and the Yahoo catalogue began as a student's attempt to catalogue the interesting places on the World Wide Web.

Students of all ages have completely different requirements from those of the business community. Whereas business looks for a way to make profit from information, students look for information for its own sake and are amongst the most prolific users of online chat services and newsgroups. Whereas business is still attempting to establish its relationship with the Internet, students already have a well-defined relationship.

This book attempts to reflect that relationship, in terms of different subjects, different levels of education and different technologies. In addition to providing a taxonomy of Web-based resources for a number of subject areas at second and third level education, it provides detailed instruction in how to find a suitable newsgroup, how to use e-mail and FTP, and looks closely at the use of the Internet at university level as a research tool, using worked examples in both arts and science disciplines.

The book can be used as a complete introduction by the novice or approached on a 'need to know' basis by advanced users. Because of the volatile nature of the Internet, I make no guarantee that the sites recommended in this book will remain available permanently. However, the sites have been chosen with stability in mind. A list of new resources will be maintained at this Web address:

http://www.unl.ac.uk/~cwright/tyi/

If you know of a resource that has proved valuable to you, please feel free to e-mail me the details at:

tyi@chroma.demon.co.uk

In the meantime, good luck with your travels!

Chris Wright

Part One
INTRODUCTION TO THE INTERNET

This section consists of two chapters which introduce the ideas and the technology behind the Internet and the tools with which you can begin to use the Internet.

Chapter 1 introduces the World Wide Web and gives an overview of the technologies upon which it is based. Understanding these technologies is helpful in that you will understand why the Internet behaves differently to a CD Rom or an ordinary computer application.

Chapter 2 introduces Web browsers and details how to get the best out of them. It also introduces the use of search engines and directories and explains how to search economically – getting the best results in the least possible time.

1 | WHAT IS THE INTERNET?

1.1 Aims of this chapter

This chapter aims to explain what the Internet is and what it is not. It will introduce a set of applications with which we will perform Internet based tasks, such as e-mail, Usenet news, file transfer protocol (FTP), Telnet, Internet Relay Chat (IRC), Web browsers and search engines. The detail of how to use these applications is given in Part Four. We will deal with connecting to the Internet from college and explain simply, what you need to do to get started. We will meet Netscape, the Web browser which will be used for many of the examples in this book. Lastly there will be a few simple exercises using a Web browser, to get you started 'surfing' the World Wide Web (WWW, or W3).

1.2 History of the Internet

The Internet is not synonymous with the WWW; although it is often used to refer to the same thing, it is as well to understand the difference. The WWW is an application that uses a protocol called HTTP (HyperText Transfer Protocol) to transfer interlinked documents consisting of text, images and computer code (Java applets) from a Web server to your desktop computer. The Internet refers to the myriad networks that are connected together which allow this transfer to take place.

The Internet runs on a layered set of protocols, commonly referred to as the TCP/IP suite. HTTP is a member of this suite, residing in the application layer along with FTP, Telnet and SMTP (e-mail) amongst others. TCP (Transmission Control Protocol) resides in the Transport layer and IP (Internet Protocol) in the Internet layer. Below this there is the Network layer which transfers data to and from the physical network attached to the computer. The protocols from Network layer to Transmission Control layer work together to provide a guaranteed delivery service for data using the protocols in the application layer. TCP provides the address of the application that the data is being sent to, for example Netscape, and IP provides the address of the network and the computer that the application is resident on.

Each network has an address – we can make a comparison with an ordinary mail address, where the network address might equate to the town, the computer address might equate to the street and the application address the house. In very simple terms, when we send data from our desktop to another computer in a different network, the data will be sent to a router (doing a job similar to a postal sorting office), which uses the IP address to determine where to send it next. This process can be done in an adaptive way so that the message will always get through; even if one route is not usable, another one will be found.

The origins of this process lie with the military's realization that communication is the key to successful campaigns, and that if the enemy manages to break the chain of command by disrupting computer networks then the war is lost. The adaptive nature of the routing process means that information can be sent by a variety of different routes as necessary, making it virtually impossible for the lines of communication to be broken. This was demonstrated by Saddam Hussein, the Iraqi leader, who during the Gulf War was able to maintain absolute secrecy as to his whereabouts, whilst maintaining control over the campaign against United Nations forces. That particular war might have ended much sooner, had the Iraqi lines of communication been successfully disrupted.

The Internet is best thought of as a number of networks, linked together. This linking makes it possible for data to travel from one place to almost anywhere. When we send an e-mail message to someone, the message travels through a number of networks before reaching its destination. Similarly, when we retrieve a page into a Web browser, the data contained by the page travels over many networks between the Web server and our PC.

1.3 What's out there?

Access to the Internet is made possible through the use of a variety of tools, each one serving a different purpose. Use of these tools will be determined by the task you have in mind.

Electronic mail (e-mail) has been widely used in education and business. The Internet makes it possible for an account holder to send and receive e-mail to/from any other account holder, anywhere on the planet, usually in a matter of seconds or minutes. This makes it faster than the post, and less intrusive than the telephone, and has swiftly become the preferred medium of communication between staff in many universities. The success of this application has probably saved more tree forests than any other computer application! E-mail is also used as the vehicle for a number of mailing lists – virtual communities grouped around a specific interest, where all mail is forwarded to all members.

The potential of the Internet is vast: apart from the military, academics were amongst the first people to put it to good use, sending one another copies of research papers in seconds, rather than the days it might take by ordinary mail. Small files may be 'attached' to e-mail messages, but sending large computer files over the network is usually done with FTP, an application layer protocol that copies a file from one computer to another and reassembles it identically at the destination. This allows us to copy papers, spreadsheets, databases, complete across a network or networks. For example, if I have a spreadsheet describing Leeds United's goal scoring record in the Premier League over the last five years, or the Dallas Cowboys' progress in the American Football League and my friend in Australia wants to ask me questions about it, it is easy for me to copy the file to an FTP server and my friend can download it and view it on her own computer.

Remote logins to computers are another activity that is made possible by the Internet. Most colleges have an online library catalogue (usually OPAC) allowing the user to log in and reserve a book or extend a loan. This is usually accomplished using the Telnet protocol, which allows the user to log in to a computer as if they were in the same room. It does not allow use of Windows style applications, but will allow the reading of e-mail and use of all programs operated from the command line.

One of the more popular Internet applications is IRC, which allows people to log in to a chat server and join a group of like minded individuals enjoying a discussion. These groups can be focused around a particular topic, or be more general, such as the various expatriate communities to be found. The nearest equivalent in real life to these groups is probably the traditional English pub, where groups of people united only by a common interest in beer indulge in conversation with friends and strangers alike.

Usenet news is supported by a network of news servers, disseminating articles under various topic specific forums called newsgroups. It is possible to find out almost any information from these groups, which are counted in thousands, ranging from conspiracy theorists to film enthusiasts, Mensa members to the Muppet show. It is impossible to describe fully the range of topics available in newsgroups, but suffice to say, if it has been thought of, even for a split second, there is probably a newsgroup devoted to it!

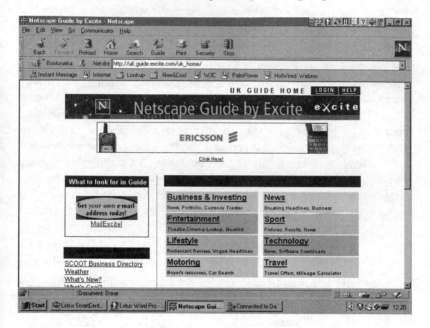

Figure 1.1 The World Wide Web (Netscape Navigator)

Without any doubt though, the most popular application on the Internet, one which has caught the imagination of the general public and business communities is the WWW. Accessed using a Web browser such as Netscape or Microsoft Explorer, the WWW allows us to view multimedia information interactively. What started out as a user friendly information service has become the focus for millions of pages bearing all kinds of data, all loosely linked together.

Every university in the world almost certainly has its own Web site – a collection of pages – and the business world is not that far behind. These pages can be searched by programs known as search engines, for references to key phrases. This allows us to perform in seconds the kind of information gathering that used to involve many hours. If I want to buy a new computer, I search the WWW for information about all the available models. Having decided which one I want, I find the nearest supplier and order it. This kind of activity is being exploited by all kinds of commercial enterprises, from supermarkets to record stores.

The WWW is a potentially useful research resource – the caveat being that there is no quality control and that Web pages are rarely permanent. The golden rule is 'Don't believe everything you read!' unless the source is verifiable.

The researcher will find much of interest – calls for conference papers are often advertised on the appropriate Usenet newsgroup, as well as the more specialized mailing lists. Journal publishers often have their own Web pages, advertising the journal and any conferences they may be sponsoring. Academics too, often publish their conference papers on the Web. Although the Web was dominated by academics, now that commerce has discovered it there is a wider range of material to search through – in particular, magazines of all types often keep a Web-accessible archive of articles. Chapters 3, 4, 5 and 6 show a variety of resources in detail, for various subject areas. Chapter 8 shows how to use the Web as a serious research tool.

The Web is also useful for other kinds of research – restaurants advertise on the Web, markets, shops, magazines and sports clubs, are all building a presence on the Web. If you are a student and new in town, you can save a small fortune by using the Web to find out where to go and what to see.

1.4 Connecting from college

To connect to the Internet from college, you will need an account on the college computer network. Many colleges allow 'open' access, typically from the library, but this is likely to be restricted to Web browsing – if you want to use other applications, you should apply to the computer services department for a network account. They will provide you with a user name and a password which you will be invited to change. Choose a word which

will be difficult for anyone to guess and change your password to it. Do
not tell anyone your password – you may find that your account is used by
a friend of a friend and if they use it to send abusive messages to someone,
you will get the blame. Technicians do not need to know your password –
they have privileged access, so there is no need to tell anyone at all.

Once you have an account, you will find that you have a small quota of
disk space. This may be used for data storage and in many colleges, to
house your own Web site. Your account should also provide you with an
e-mail address. If it does not, you may register with one of the 'free' e-
mail servers such as Hotmail

http://www.hotmail.com/

which allows anyone to hold an account under a name of their own
choosing, which they can access from anywhere in the world. For the
purposes of this book, we will assume that your account is on a Novell or
Windows NT network – Unix account holders will have all the same
facilities which will work in much the same way, only the interface for
applications is likely to be different.

When you approach a computer in college, you should see a screen
containing a login dialogue. Simply enter your user name and password in
the appropriate box and in a few seconds you should find yourself looking
at the familiar Windows style desktop. On the desktop, there should be an
icon for Internet Explorer or Netscape Navigator. Clicking on this icon
should result in the Web browser appearing and displaying your university
or college Web site.

1.5 Surfing the Web

When you look at the document contained in the Web browser, you will
see that certain phrases or words appear underlined and in a different colour
(usually blue) to the rest of the text. These phrases are links to other pages
– if you move the mouse over one of these phrases and click the left hand
button, you will move to the page indicated by the phrase. Clicking on
'Music' in the page in Figure 1.2, takes you to a page detailing some of
my favourite CDs (see Figure 1.3).

Clicking on 'Programming the Internet' in Figure 1.2 takes you to a page
describing one of the courses I teach at the University of North London.

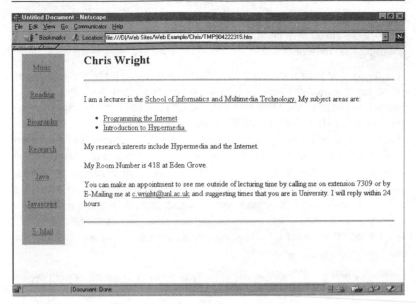

Figure 1.2 The author's home page

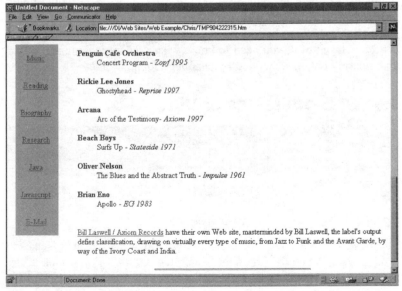

Figure 1.3 The author's music page

You may also find that certain graphics are 'clickable'; you can easily tell because the cursor will change to a pointing finger when you move it over anything that may be a link.

It is likely that your university or college Web site will feature a menu of some kind, indicating the main areas of interest. You will find that the pages contained in the Web site will be arranged in a hierarchy, like the roots of a tree. It will start with a few options and each link will lead on to other pages until it reaches a logical end point. For example a link entitled 'Faculties' may lead to a page listing all the faculties and schools in the university. Clicking on one of the school links will take you to a page dedicated to a particular school, which may contain a list of staff. Clicking on a lecturer's name may take you to their own Web page which may contain a list of their interests. Clicking on one of these interests may take you outside the university altogether, at which point you are 'Surfing the Internet'.

Surfing or browsing describes the activity of following whatever path seems interesting, with no particular destination in mind. This is both a strength and a weakness of the Internet. It is a strength because some fascinating 'journeys' can be made by simply pointing and clicking, but a weakness because this type of activity is rarely rewarding, except in entertainment value. The WWW can be compared to cable television in the sense that to get the best out of it, you need to know what you are looking for, rather than missing out on something by channel hopping.

1.6 Web addresses or URLs

Figure 1.4 Netscape Navigator controls

The location bar is a field, found in the top third of the screen in Netscape and Microsoft Explorer. The field is labelled 'Go to:'. If you look at the location bar, you will see that it contains a series of words, in the format

http://www.aPlace.aDomain.aCountry/aDirectory/aFile.html

This is known as a Uniform Resource Locator (URL). This is effectively the Web address of the page described in the file **aFile.html**.

- The first part, **http**, identifies the protocol used by the browser.
- The second part, **www**, identifies the computer acting as a Web server.
- **anInstitution.aDomain.aCountry** identifies the network, usually mapping on to the name and type of the organization owning the network. **aCountry** identifies the country where that network is located.
- **aDirectory** identifies the location of a directory on the Web server containing HTML pages and lastly, **aFile.html** identifies a particular page.
- **www.anInstitution.aDomain.aCountry** maps on to an IP address which is represented as a number in dotted decimal format, for example 135.250.254.1. It is a lot easier to remember a phrase than a number, hence the use of words in the location bar. We can leave it to the computer to translate the words to numbers – this is done by a Domain Name Service (DNS) Lookup.

A little more detail can be gleaned from the address. The type of organization – **ac** or **edu** will indicate that the organization is a college or university, **co** or **com** indicate a commercial enterprise, **org** indicates a non-commercial enterprise, **gov** a government department, **net** a network provider etc. The country is usually indicated in the last part of the network identifier, the exception to this is America, where the country is left out. Country codes are quite simple to decipher:

Australia	au	
Canada	ca	
Finland	fi	
Germany	de	(Deutschland)
Greece	gr	
Hong Kong	hk	
Ireland	ie	
Japan	jp	
Netherlands	nl	
Spain	es	(Espana)
United Kingdom	uk	

Knowing the country can be useful if, for example, you are confronted with a list of 'mirror' sites (the same site, duplicated over a number of servers is said to be mirrored). Always choose the nearest geographical location, or one in a country where it is the middle of the night. The first option is common sense – it keeps traffic off the network; the second is an option if a particular server is busy (i.e. taking a long time to respond).

These conventions are guidelines only. However, a new addressing system is being implemented which will allow other types of address, thus blurring the boundaries between these easily identifiable addresses. The reason for this is the incredible growth rate of the Internet – it is literally running out of addresses, so new addressing systems must be employed to prevent any two organisations having the same address.

1.7 Web resources

C-Net: The Computer Network

http://www.cnet.com/

One of the first and most successful magazine style sites. C-Net is primarily concerned with computers and is mandatory viewing for anyone interested in technology. Presented in an attractive and accessible format, the content is usually excellent in terms of relevance, but rarely probes beyond the surface.

Netscape: What's Cool

http://uk.guide.excite.com/uk_home/whats_cool.dcg

In the beginning, before the WWW took off, and the only graphically aware browsers available were Mosaic and Netscape, the What's Cool site was a must visit for groundbreaking designs, interesting content and the plain weird. Nowadays the Web is too big to monitor accurately and this site is no longer the compulsory viewing it once was. It is though, still a good place to set off from.

Netscape: NetCenter

http://www.netscape.com/

The Netscape NetCenter is the place to visit if you are interested in the WWW's development and maintenance.

Microsoft: Home Pages

http://www.Microsoft.com/

Love 'em or hate 'em, you can't ignore them! Their Web site is always state-of-the-art and contains some excellent demonstrations of new Microsoft technologies such as their XML parser and ActiveX controls.

Life on the Internet

http://www.screen.com/start/guide/default.html

Excellent magazine style site, containing essentially a beginner's guide, explaining many Internet applications and containing links to 'How To's', Style Guides etc.

1.8 Summary

The resources covered by the word Internet can be found in a number of areas – mailing lists (Listserv), newsgroups (Usenet), Telnet (libraries) and the WWW.

After reading this chapter, you should have or be in the process of getting, a user name for your college network. You should be able to describe the function of Usenet news, e-mail, FTP and the World Wide Web.

We have covered a little of the history of the Internet and you should be able to describe in general terms the functionality of the TCP/IP protocol suite. You should know the difference between an IP address and a URL, and by looking at a URL, should be able to deduce what country the resource is located in and what type of resource it is.

The list of Web resources represents a sample of the kind of sites you might find useful as you begin to master the art of surfing the Net.

1.9 Exercises

1 Starting at your college home page, draw a map, including all the links from pages that you do not click, which describes a journey spanning five links. The resulting diagram should resemble the roots of a tree.

2 Find the page for your own school within the college and

write down the path you took to get there (i.e.which pages did you pass through).

3 Compare this with the map you drew in question 1. How do you think the two are related?

2 | THE WORLD WIDE WEB

2.1 Aims of this chapter

This chapter will introduce the WWW standards and explain why it is necessary to have independent standards. It will introduce the use of Web browsers and detail the major types of Web browser available in colleges and universities. The effective compilation of Internet bookmarks will be covered, the use of search engines will be discussed and the major differences between the search facilities available will be explained. Each search engine covered is tested on the basis of searching for a name and a specific resource; comments concerning the quality of a search resource are based around these tests. The rules governing simple and advanced searches using various search engines will be covered.

2.2 Standards

The WWW was invented by Tim Berners-Lee. It is a system based upon the HTTP protocol, whereby documents consisting of various media types may be transported from a Web server to a Web browser operating on a computer connected to a network, anywhere in the world. These documents are specified using a language called HTML (HyperText Mark-up Language) which is interpreted by the browser to define the layout of the text, images and embedded programs which make up the document. HTML is currently standardized on version 4.0 and it is thought that it has now reached maturity and will not be subject to the radical alterations that have characterized its progress so far.

HTML is derived from SGML, the language that underpins the word processor. It works by attaching tags to portions of text which are interpreted by the browser to define layout information, for example:

<B>	Bold
<I>	Italic
<P>	New paragraph
** **	Line break
<IMG>	Image

Part of a simple Web page, written in HTML would look like this:

```
<HTML>
<BODY BGCOLOR= "white">
<B> Welcome to a Very Simple Web Page </B>
<P>They don't come any simpler
</BODY>
</HTML>
```

This Web page contains a few very simple **<I>** *tags* **</I>**, designed mainly to influence the layout of the page, such as <BODY> and <P>.

It is not within the scope of this book to cover HTML in full; there is an excellent introduction to HTML in this series, *Teach Yourself HTML*, written by Mac Bride, which does that job admirably. The tags described give an idea of the type of control over presentation that the language gives to the author of HTML documents. What is missing, is a set of logical descriptive tags which allow us to categorize information by type. This meta information, which makes searching documents much more economical is supplied by a language called XML (Extensible Mark-up Language) which allows us to use programmer defined tags enabling us to define the data contained in a document in terms of its content, rather than what it should look like, for example:

```
<AUTHOR>
<ABSTRACT>
<EXERCISES>
```

In the context of this book, such tags could be used to allow a search engine to return with the abstract only of the book, or to search a publisher's Web site to retrieve the abstracts of all books written by Chris Wright.

XML will be supported in new versions of Microsoft Explorer and Netscape, available in late 1998.

With this proliferation of languages available for deployment over the WWW, it is necessary to have some kind of agreed, definitive standard.

This is supplied by the W3 Committee, whose Web pages at **http://www.w3.org/** provide news of the current standards and those in development, as well as details of various research projects. The alternative is to have commercial interests provide a *de facto* standard, which in the case of Microsoft and Netscape, has contributed to a situation where browsers have to support different implementations of languages. The result of this is that we can never be quite certain that our pages are viewed in the way that we designed them to be.

2.3 Browsers

A Web browser is a computer program that uses the HTTP protocol to retrieve Web pages from a Web server, and displays them in a human readable form. The first graphical browser was called Mosaic, and the designers went on to form the Netscape Corporation which gives us Netscape Navigator. At the time of writing, there are only two significant players in the browser field, Netscape and Microsoft. This is largely because both companies have elected to give the browser away free via the Internet, from the parent companies' Web sites. Both of these browsers are marketed as part of a software suite, giving the user e-mail and news readers and authoring tools to create Web pages.

2.3.1 Netscape Navigator

The interface of Netscape Navigator is shown in Figure 2.1. It is divided into a large viewing area, in which the Web pages are viewed and a number of tool bars which are customizable by the user.

The most important tool bar is the location bar, in which the URL of the current page is displayed. URLs can be entered directly into the location bar if known; pressing the return key on the computer keyboard tells the browser to retrieve the page from the location described in the toolbar. You will also notice that the toolbar has a pull-down menu. This retains the address of every URL entered directly into the location bar, giving the user a short cut to retrieving a recently visited resource.

The status bar displays useful information describing the status of a current download. For example, the size of the file, the percentage currently downloaded and the transfer speed in bytes per second. This area is also accessible by Web pages using JavaScript, so occasionally a message pertinent to the current Web page is displayed there.

Navigation bar   Location bar

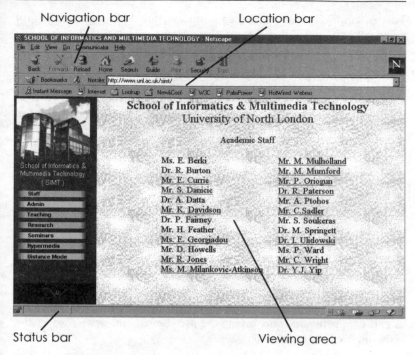

Status bar   Viewing area

Figure 2.1 Netscape Navigator

The navigation bar contains a set of buttons allowing the user to go back and forward, to and from the previously visited page, to go straight to a user defined home page, to invoke a search engine and to display the security status of the current page. The browser records a history of visits in the current session, so the back button allows the user to step back through this history incrementally.

Clicking on the View menu allows the user to show or hide any one of these toolbars. This is useful if we want to maximize the viewing area in order, for example, to view a painting.

2.3.2 Microsoft Explorer

The interface for Microsoft Explorer is arranged almost identically to Netscape Navigator. This incarnation of the interface was pioneered by Microsoft – as the battle for supremacy shifted from the version of HTML supported, towards the additional functionality supported by the browser, the interfaces moved much closer together as much of the functionality is identical. However, there is one considerable difference – behind the interface, Microsoft have integrated the browser with the operating system itself, making the software significantly faster to load, and offering the opportunity to browse through files on the client computer seamlessly with those on the Internet.

Microsoft has also pioneered the use of XML in Web browsers – the current version includes an XML parser which allows the browser to support the Document Object Model used by Microsoft to enable scripting languages to access locations within a page. This for example allows animation to be implemented using 'Dynamic HTML' in which the document exhibits a limited amount of interactivity, responding to the position of the mouse in pre-scripted fashion. Netscape's implementation of Dynamic HTML differs from the Explorer version, so pages may behave differently in each browser.

2.4 Bookmark files

Bookmarks give us a way of saving shortcuts to pages we will want to visit again. Both the main browsers support bookmarks, which are stored in HTML files. With a little planning, structured sets of bookmarks can be created, which in the latest release of Netscape, may be linked to your network user name and so will be accessible from any computer in college. It is less convenient, but still practical, in earlier versions of Netscape, to import a bookmark file from a floppy disk.

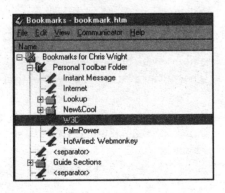

Figure 2.2 Bookmarks in Netscape Navigator

To organize bookmarks in Netscape Navigator (see Figure 2.2), simply click on the Bookmarks menu to the left of the location bar and choose 'Edit Bookmarks'. This will display your bookmark file as a hierarchy of folders in the viewer window. Right clicking on a file or folder will display a menu which allows the user to create and name a new folder (inside the one clicked on), a new separator (above the file or folder clicked upon) or to delete bookmarks and folders.

One way to organize bookmarks is to set up a hierarchy of interests and allocate particular locations to different folders. For example, we could divide our interests into recreational and academic folders. In the recreational folder we could have subfolders – Sport, Computer Games and Music, for example. The academic branch could be split into subject folders.

To save a bookmark, navigate to the page you want to save, click on the bookmarks menu and choose 'File Bookmark' (choosing 'Save Bookmark' will save the link at the top level which we do not want to do for reasons explained later). A submenu will appear which allows the user to point to the folder in which the link is to be saved.

Since bookmarks are saved serially it is possible for a short list to metamorphose into a sprawling Web of locations in the space of a couple of sessions. If the structure of the bookmark file has been thought through, it is the work of a second to place the link into the appropriate folder. It may take a little longer to track down a saved link in a single list of hundreds!

2.5 Search engines, directories and libraries

There are a number of tools available on the Web that make it easier for us to find information economically. Broadly, these tools can be divided into three categories.

Search engines use an automated method of searching documents, usually some kind of agent software or Web robot to visit a Web page and create a record in the search engine's index, based on a sample of the full text, the meta tags indicated in the header or the links that point to a page. The user interface of a search engine will usually allow searching by keywords and Boolean operators (AND, OR, NOT).

Directories are hierarchically organized indexes of subject categories that allow the user to browse through lists of Web sites by category, in search of relevant information. The compilation of these directories is done by humans, which means that the references retrieved will be more closely tied to the subject, but they will be based on a smaller pool of sites.

Libraries are highly specialized directories. They work on the same principle, but the references are likely to be of a higher quality in research terms than those returned from an ordinary directory. These will be based on an even smaller number of sites and will often contain meta-indexes, pointing to other libraries.

These categories are responsive to different types of search. If we need to track down every reference to a highly specific phrase such as a name, then a search engine such as AltaVista would be the most appropriate tool to use. If the intention is to assemble a number of topic specific resources then a directory such as Yahoo would be more appropriate. When we need to assemble material to research an academic project, a library such as the WWW Virtual Library (discussed in depth on page 32) would be ideal.

Successful Web searching depends on using the appropriate resources. This table recommends the best resource to use for various types of search.

Type of search	Resource
Overview	Yahoo (directory)
Point me in the right direction	Excite (search engine, includes summary)
Pinpoint	AltaVista (search engine)
Media type (image, sound, plugin)	HotBot (search engine)
Natural language	Infoseek (search engine)
Name	AltaVista, Infoseek (search engine)
Internet domain (.ac, .com)	HotBot (eearch engine)
Browse	Yahoo (directory)
Research papers	WWW Virtual Library, Argus Clearinghouse (library)

2.5.1 AltaVista
http://www.altavista.com

AltaVista claims to index all existing Web pages by full text. This makes it arguably the most comprehensive resource on the Web. Unfortunately, this is also one of its biggest disadvantages – the returns to simple queries are often numbered in thousands. To get the best out of AltaVista, we should use advanced queries in order to narrow the field of the search. This means using Boolean operators to force includes and excludes. The syntax for typical advanced queries is given below:

"Oliver Cromwell" AND "English Civil War"

This query will return documents including both phrases, defined within quotation marks.

Football AND NOT Association

will return documents referring to Football, but excluding all documents referring to the English professional game.

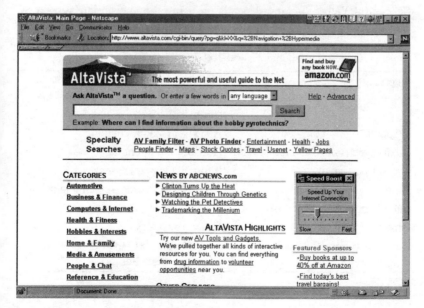

Figure 2.3 The AltaVista search engine

("John Lennon" OR "Paul McCartney") AND "composed by"

will return song titles composed by either of these two people.

(Goldfish OR Carp) AND NOT "Ornamental Ponds"

will return documents referring to these fish, excluding those documents referring to Ornamental Ponds.

Phrases and names must be placed in quotes, or each word will be treated independently – for example, we should search for **"Mary Queen of Scots"** rather than **Mary Queen of Scots** since there are a lot of Marys out there! Brackets are not compulsory, but help the user to define the logic of a compound search.

AltaVista currently provides the most comprehensive index to the Internet, including newsgroups, name searches and references to URLs.

2.5.2 Yahoo

http://www.yahoo.com

Yahoo is unquestionably the most popular directory on the Web. It is most useful for general searching by category, and allows the user to browse through series of directories grouped by topic. The original intention was to include only 'good' Web sites, although whether this means good by design or good by information content remains unclear.

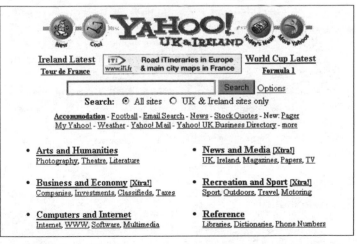

Figure 2.4 Yahoo Directory

The interface for Yahoo, a portion of which is shown in Figure 2.4, contains a list of generalized headings that start the user off on a journey through the directory. There is also a search engine that has the benefit of returning results from categories the user may not at first have thought of looking at.

The Yahoo search options allow the user to carry out Boolean searches using AND/OR and +/− to indicate inclusion or exclusion.

Yahoo perfectly encapsulates the 'browsing' ethos of the WWW. It is possible to turn up all sorts of weird and wonderful Web sites via Yahoo, ranging from the perfectly pointless to the genuinely informative.

2.5.3 Infoseek

http://www.infoseek.com

Infoseek is possibly an even more powerful search engine than AltaVista. Its index includes images, newsgroups, FAQs, e-mail addresses and even telephone numbers. Boolean searches may be carried out using the + and − operators instead of AND and NOT, and brackets to include a phrase.

Examples of typical queries are:

   (Oliver Cromwell) + (English Civil War)

This will return documents including both phrases defined within brackets.

   Football − Association

will return documents referring to Football, but excluding all documents referring to the English professional game.

Like many of the newer search facilities, Infoseek maintains a directory based interface similar to Yahoo, as well as a conventional search engine, allowing the user the opportunity to search by browsing as well as by keyword. The interface is fully regionalized, allowing the user the opportunity to restrict a search to a location or the entire Web. In tests, despite its claims, Infoseek UK returned a significantly smaller number of resources than AltaVista.

2.5.4 HotBot

http://www.hotbot.com

HotBot is another hybrid search engine/directory. It is run by *Wired* magazine and sports a superb user interface, allowing the user to choose

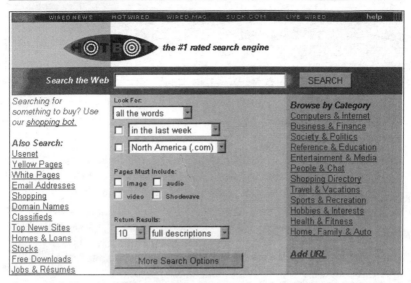

Figure 2.5 The HotBot search engine. Copyright (c) 1994-98 Wired Digital, Inc. all Rights Reserved

various categories restricting the search, via pull down menus, in addition to supporting the usual Boolean searches (see Figure 2.5).

Tests returned pleasingly focused matches extremely quickly. In fact this was undoubtedly the fastest resource locator on the day, though as this is one of the newer search facilities and does not yet boast the user base of AltaVista and Infoseek this is only to be expected.

2.5.5 Argus Clearinghouse

http://www.clearinghouse.com

The Argus Clearinghouse is a meta-library (library of libraries), originally created by the library at the University of Michigan, containing pointers to resources grouped initially into thirteen categories: Arts & Humanities, Business & Employment, Communication, Computers & Information Technology, Education, Engineering, Environment, Government & Law, Health & Medicine, Places & Peoples, Recreation, Science & Mathematics and finally Social Sciences & Social Issues.

Clicking on any one of these categories allows the user to access a number of subcategories each of which leads on to a keyword based search. The search eventually resolves into a reference to an external site or sites, itself a gateway to other topic specific resources. Each site is meticulously graded in terms of its design, organization and ease of searching.

2.5.6 How to search economically

Searching economically means getting the best value for your time. You should decide in advance what type of search best suits your purpose and allocate a suitable amount of time.

Browsing through directories takes time; the benefit lies in the serendipity factor, where a resource is discovered almost by accident. The more precise the search, the more likely you are to get the result you are looking for and the time consumed will be minimized. For this type of searching use search engines. For academic use, libraries or 'gateway' sites represent the best value and the most reliable information – remember, in the absence of quality control, the library sites are the nearest thing to guaranteed reliability available.

2.6 Summary

After reading this chapter, you should be familiar with the two main Web browsers, Netscape Navigator and Internet Explorer. You should know the value of bookmark files and be able to create your own hierarchically arranged bookmarks. You should be able to differentiate between the World Wide Web and the Internet and you should be able to carry out an Internet search with the most appropriate search facility.

2.7 Exercises

1 Locate the W3 committee Web site and find out about 'Amaya'.

2 Create a folder in your bookmarks called 'HTML' and save a link to this page in it.

3 Load your college home page, and try to locate your own school pages by clicking on the available links.

4 What search mechanism would you use to discover information about:

a) Beekeeping in North Yorkshire?

b) Picasso's 'blue' period?

c) Restaurants in central London, England?

d) Industrial Music?

e) Other Web sites containing links to your college pages?

f) Research papers discussing Herman Melville's *Moby Dick*?

5 Using AltaVista, create an advanced query to return resources on the composer John Cale, documenting his time as a member of the Velvet Underground.

6 Using the Argus Clearinghouse, find out which film star has the most Web pages devoted to him or her.

7 Use AltaVista to search for references to your own name – you may be surprised by the result!

8 Use different search engines for an identical search.

a) Which one is fastest?

b) Which one returns the most irrelevant resources?

c) Which one returns the most useful resources first?

Part Two
THE INTERNET RESOURCES

This part of the book deals with distinct subject areas; Humanities; Art, Archaeology and Architecture; Business, Environmental and Social Studies and the Sciences.

Each area includes a close look at resources providing a gateway to more specialized resources, as well as a review of some of the sites offering specialised information in a particular subject area

Before we involve ourselves in specialist subject areas, there are two specialist academic gateway sites that should always be included in any research exercise.

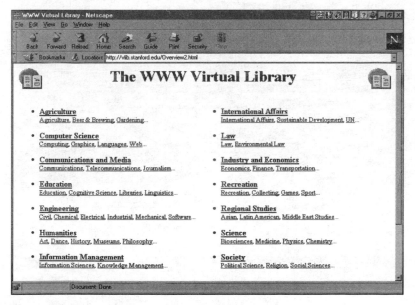

Figure Two.1 The WWW Virtual Library

The WWW Virtual Library
http://www.vlib.org/

The WWW Virtual Library is the oldest catalogue of the Web, started by Tim Berners-Lee, the creator of the Web itself. It is a distributed application, run by a loose confederation of volunteers from academia, who compile pages of key links for particular areas in which they are expert; these specialist areas are hosted on various servers all over the world. Vitally for academic purposes, this arrangement ensures quality control with the result that the Virtual Library pages are widely recognized as being amongst the highest-quality guides to particular sections of the Web.

The address given above is the official address for the Virtual Library; however, it is mirrored in several locations, listed at this site. For practical purposes, it is advisable to bookmark the mirror site which is geographically closest to you.

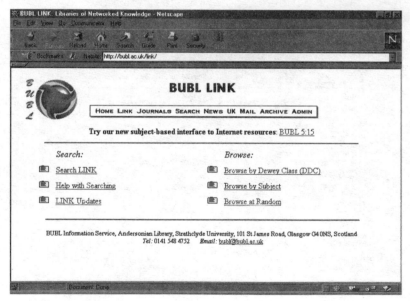

Figure Two.2 BUBL Link

BUBL Link

http://link.bubl.ac.uk/

BUBL is a national information service for the higher education community, funded by JISC, the Joint Information Systems Committee of the Higher Education Funding Councils of England, Scotland and Wales and the Department of Education for Northern Ireland. BUBL is located and run from the Andersonian library of the University of Strathclyde, Glasgow, Scotland. Much more than a directory of resources, BUBL provides the following services:

BUBL Link: catalogue of selected Internet resources

BUBL Journals: abstracts, full text, hundreds of titles

BUBL Search: search BUBL or beyond

BUBL News: jobs, events, surveys, updates

BUBL UK: the UK home page

BUBL Mail: mailing lists and mail archives

BUBL Archive: LIS (Library and Information Science), journals, Internet development

3 | HUMANITIES

3.1 Aims of this chapter

The humanities are particularly well served on the World Wide Web. In this chapter we will look at the main gateways into resources for each subject heading. We will not be using the major search engines described earlier (see section 2.5), but using known Web sites carrying subject specific materials or links. A review of a selection of interesting resources will be given, all of which can be accessed through one or other of these gateway sites.

3.2 Humanities gateways

HUMBUL

http://users.ox.ac.uk/~humbul/

HUMBUL, like the WWW Virtual Library is a vast resource, centred around collections of high quality links to scholarly resources. It focuses exclusively on the Humanities, and is run by Chris Stephens at Oxford University.

Voice of the Shuttle

http://humanitas.ucsb.edu/

Voice of the Shuttle is perhaps the most comprehensive Humanities oriented resource available. Maintained by Professor Alan Liu at the University of California, Santa Barbara, it lists journals, mailing lists and newsgroups, conferences and calls for papers under each item in a directory tree that is easily navigable, yet leads to literally thousands of high quality Web resources.

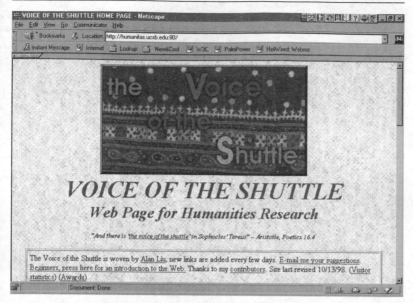

Figure 3.1 Voice of the Shuttle

Humanities Hub

http://www.gu.edu.au/gwis/hub/

Maintained by Anita Greenhill and Gordon Fletcher at the Faculty of Arts,
Griffith University, Brisbane, Australia, Humanities Hub offers a range of
high quality resources for the Humanities, including subject specialized
chat forums.

History/Social Studies Web Site for K12 Teachers

http://www.execpc.com/~dboals/boals.html

K12 is a Web site aimed at promoting the use of the Internet as a teaching
resource. There are links to many subject areas available, many of which
have been chosen because of their stimulating qualities as teaching
resources. This is a particularly good resource for secondary level students
and teachers.

3.3 History

The majority of history resources on the WWW are concerned with American and British history, with a slight emphasis on military history. There are also many sites dealing with social and economic history and many of the gateway sites mentioned here categorize European history and Eastern history separately.

3.3.1 History gateways

Rutgers University

http://www.libraries.rutgers.edu/rulib/socsci/hist/amhist.html

The Web resources (see Figure 3.1) are categorized by both time period (e.g. 16th Century) and type (e.g. maps, statistics, treaties, electronic journals, etc.).

HORUS

http://www.ucr.edu/h-gig/horuslinks.html

An extensive resource from the University of California which deals with history from many perspectives, including antiquarian, architectural and art.

HUMBUL

http://users.ox.ac.uk/~humbul

See page 35 and Figure 3.3.

The Library of Congress

http://lcweb.loc.gov/homepage/lchp.html

This resource is also accessible by Telnet at **locis.loc.gov** and contains amongst other things extensive collections of speeches, the text of the American Constitution, Declaration of Independence and links to the Libraries gopher system **marvel.loc.gov**.

Internet Modern History Sourcebook

http://www.fordham.edu/halsall/mod/modsbook.html

Extensive resource containing links to FTP sites and library catalogues as well as Web pages and image archives. Well worth a visit even for the non-historian.

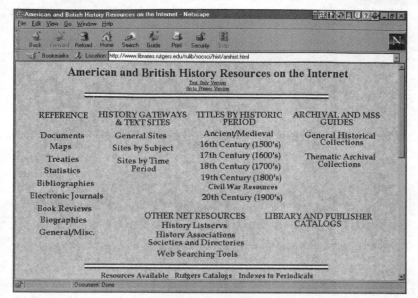

Figure 3.2 Rutgers University History Index

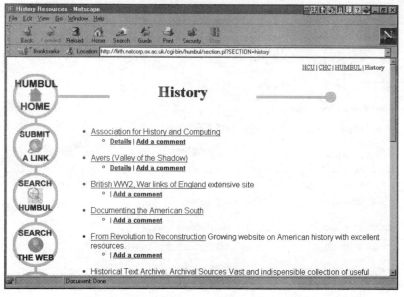

Figure 3.3 HUMBUL

3.3.2 History bookmarks

The following sites represent a mere fraction of the resources accessible through the gateway sites listed above. They represent a cross-section of material that may be of interest to historians at all levels.

American Memory Project

http://rs6.loc.gov/amtitle.html

A marvellous graphic resource, containing thousands of pictures cataloguing American history and culture. Examples range from the American Civil War to the Great Depression and also include famous cultural icons such as Marilyn Monroe.

The Era of the Spanish Galleons

http://www.northlink.com/~hauxe/

This site is full of detail about the life of sailors on board the Spanish Treasure ships that carried gold and treasure from the New World back to Spain. It gives an account of the 'Voyage of Misery' suffered by a fleet sailing from Vera Cruz to Spain via Havana. Dogged by misfortune from

Figure 3.4 The Marx/Engels Internet Archive

the very beginning, one ship survived disease, storms and a plague of starving rats before being captured by Dutch pirates within view of the Spanish coast!

The Catapult Museum Online

http://www.nzp.com/02contents.html

For those interested in military history, this site is dedicated to the development and use of the catapult as a weapon of war. Immaculately researched and illustrated the site covers mainly ancient and medieval history, for obvious reasons.

The Marx/Engels Internet Archive

http://www.marx.org/

A fascinating site, containing photographs, documents and articles concerning Marx, Engels and the rise of Marxism. Essential viewing for anyone researching the background to modern Russian history.

The Italian Renaissance

http://pw2.netcom.com/~giardina/italian.html

Authoritative collection of articles and documents chronicling the Italian Renaissance. This site would be useful to Art Historians and students at second and third level education.

3.4 Media Studies and Film

Web-based resources for media studies are generally divided into smaller domains than the overarching history sites described in section 3.3. Film oriented sites are plentiful, but usually amount to little more than lists. The best and most wide reaching sites are featured here.

3.4.1 Media Studies gateways

ScreenSite

http://www.tcf.ua.edu/ScreenSite/

This site is a film studies gateway in the truest sense of the word. It contains sections dedicated to research, conferences (including lists of forthcoming conferences), production (including film festivals and available grants)

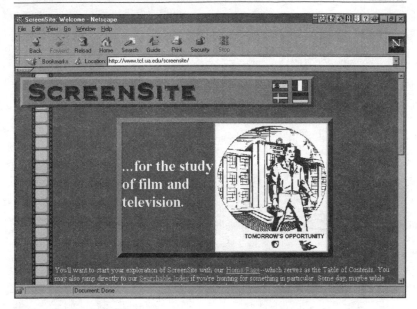

Figure 3.5 ScreenSite

and lists of useful links. It is also multilingual, providing versions in all the major European languages.

HUMBUL (See page 35)

http://users.ox.ac.uk/~humbul/

Voice of the Shuttle (See page 35)

http://humanitas.ucsb.edu/

MCS (See page 71)

http://www.aber.ac.uk/~dgc/mcs.html

SOFIA

http://www.unl.ac.uk/sofia/index.html

SOFIA started life as a student project in 1996 and has evolved to become one of the most interesting film resources on the WWW. Apart from the SOFIA Links page, the site contains pages dedicated to film theory, camerawork, script writing etc. There are e-mail discussion groups covering

a selection of subjects ranging from employment to film noir and Java
applets bringing you quotes from famous movie directors!

3.4.2 Media Studies bookmarks

The WWW is swiftly becoming a recognized medium in its own right, so
in addition to Media Studies resources such as the Virginia Newspaper
project and the Internet Movie Database, included here is a selection of
the kind of cutting edge Web sites that could be of interest to humanities
students.

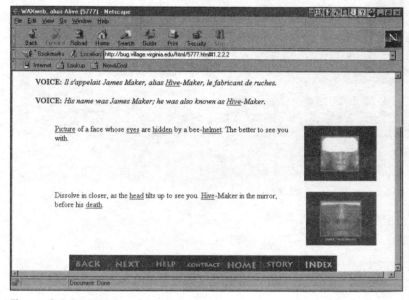

Figure 3.6 WaxWeb

WaxWeb

http://bug.village.virginia.edu/

A genuinely evolutionary Web site, WaxWeb is an experiment in the
construction of narrative by collaboration – part film, part photography,
part book and expanding rapidly. It makes interesting viewing if you have
the appropriate plug-ins to view film clips.

William Burroughs

http://199.0.70.23/~brooklyn/People/WilliamSBurroughs.html

One of the few writers who can realistically claim to have pre-empted hypertext. There are a number of Web sites celebrating the author's life. This is the most complete.

ADA Project

http://www.cs.yale.edu/HTML/YALE/CS/HyPlans/tap/tap.html

Named after Augusta Ada Byron, the Countess Lovelace, who was the most influential woman in computing in the nineteenth century. She was Lord Byron's daughter and instrumental in the design of the all mechanical Difference Engine which is generally considered to be the forerunner of the modern electronic computer. The ADA Project is concerned with the gender issues surrounding women in computing, which until recently was seen as a primarily male occupation.

Virginia Newspaper Project – The Sinking of the Titanic

http://vsla.edu/vnp/titanic/titanic1.html

A fascinating site concerned with the newspaper coverage of the Titanic disaster. Contains reproductions of newspaper articles published at the time as well as a thorough analysis of the way the event was portrayed in the American media.

The Internet Movie Database

http://www.uk.imdb.com/

If you need to find out anything at all about a film, this is the site to visit. Each film has links to Web sites, lists of articles, script information, location details, cast lists etc.

Bladerunner

http://www.uq.edu.au/~csmchapm/bladerunner/products-pub.html

Links to conference and journal papers based on the influential movie and Philip K Dick's book *Do Androids Dream of Electric Sheep* on which the film was based.

India Bollywood

http://www.indiabollywood.com/

A superb site chronicling and celebrating the Indian film industry, which in terms of numbers of films produced is considerably larger than Hollywood.

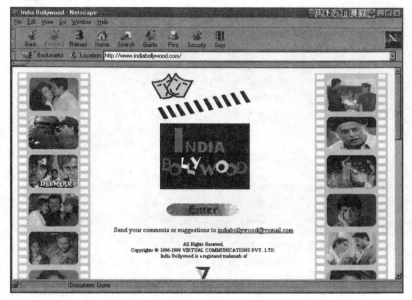

Figure 3.7 Bollywood

3.5 English Literature

English Literature is served by an abundance of gateway sites, particularly in the United States. Critical Theory and the Classics are well represented and more modern nuances such as Science Fiction and Cyberculture are beginning to make their presence felt.

3.5.1 English Literature gateways

Voice of the Shuttle

http://humanitas.ucsb.edu/

Ranks alongside specialist English servers as a definitive English Literature gateway. (See page 35.)

Oxford University Internet Resources for English
http://www.english.ox.ac.uk/compute/internet.html

Created by Claire Warwick and Chris Stephens, this resource contains links to various resources, including mailing lists, external and internal Web sites (e.g. the Bodleian Library).

Figure 3.8 Oxford University English Department

HUMBUL
http://users.ox.ac.uk/~humbul/

Well worth a look, this resource values quality over quantity.

(See page 35.)

The English Server
http://www.eserver.org/

The English Server is based at Carnegie Mellon University and is organized in a very traditional directory style.

One of the most comprehensive listings around, the links are arranged

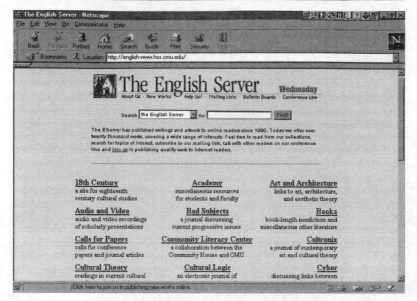

Figure 3.9 The English Server at Carnegie Mellon University

into a number of categories which include:

- 18th Century: a site for eighteenth-century cultural studies
- Art and Architecture: links to Art, Architecture and Aesthetic theory
- Bad Subjects: a journal discussing current progressive issues
- Calls for Papers: calls for conference papers and journal articles
- Cultronix: a journal of contemporary art and cultural theory
- Cultural Theory: readings in current cultural studies and critical theory
- Cultural Logic: an electronic journal of Marxist theory and practice
- Cyber: discussing links between technology and culture
- Drama: a collection of plays, modern works and classics
- Feminism: select resources in feminism and women's studies
- Fiction: novels and short fiction, classics and new works

- Film and Television: works in film, television and other media studies
- Gender and Sexuality: resources concerning gender, sex and sexuality
- Languages: resources in language studies and theory
- Libraries: links to international catalogues
- Literacy and Education: resources for both students and teachers
- Marx and Engels: a collection of writings in economic and social theory
- Philosophy: writings by modern and classical philosophers
- Poetry: original and classic verse, literary and poetic theory
- Rhetoric: scholarly and pedagogical resources for rhetoricians
- Sudden: original poetry that reflects imagination and intelligence

Literary Resources on the Net

http://www.english.upenn.edu/~jlynch/Lit/

Maintained by Jack Lynch at the University of Pennsylvania, this is a useful selection of links divided into categories including: Classical & Biblical, Medieval, Renaissance, Eighteenth century, Romantic, Victorian British, Twentieth Century British and Irish, American, Theatre and Drama, Theory, Women's Literature and feminism, Ethnicities and nationalities, Hypertext.

MIT Library Literature Resources

http://libraries.mit.edu/humanities/Literature/

The MIT site divides its interests into the following classifications leading to self contained sites: Classical and Medieval Literature, 16th–19th Century Literature, Twentieth Century Literature, American and Canadian Literature, Drama and Poetry, Women and Culture.

Also featured are links to broader classifications such as: Literary Works in Full Text, Specific Authors or Works, Electronic Journals.

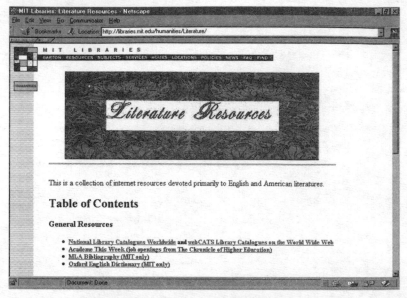

Figure 3.10 MIT Library Literature Resources

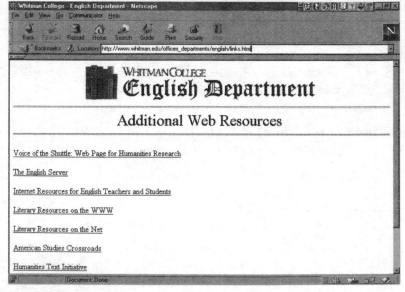

Figure 3.11 Whitman College English Department

Whitman College English Department

http://www.whitman.edu/offices_departments/english/links.html

The Whitman College resources link to a number of other gateway sites including the ubiquitous Voice of the Shuttle and the English Server, but also contains a list of 100 English Departments, many of which in turn provide their own resources.

Missing Pages

http://www.Colorado.EDU/English/mispag/

Quoting E.M.Forster: 'Only Connect' in the introductory banner, this is a lively selection of links, maintained by Mary Klages at Colorado University. The contents page contains links to resources in the areas of: Critical Theory and Cultural Studies, Drama, Eighteenth-Century Studies, Feminism and Women's Studies, English Server Fiction Collection, Film and Television, Gender and Sexuality, Government, Law and Society, History, Journals, Languages and Linguistics, Literacy and Education, Marx and Engels' Writings, Philosophy, Poetry, Race, Rhetoric.

Figure 3.12 Missing Pages

D. Diane Davis Critical/Cultural Theory Links
http://www.odu.edu/gmusers/davis/crit.htm

Almost uniquely amongst literary sites, D. Diane Davis' pages show a sense of humour, manifest in a site which is accessible, enjoyable and informal, decorated with wacky visuals, but none the less containing links to a range of valuable resources, including specialized sites on Heidegger, Nietzsche and Baudrillard as well as, more generally, cyberculture, MOOs and online journals.

3.5.2 English Literature bookmarks

Resources for studying *Beowulf*
http://www.georgetown.edu/irvinemj/english016/beowulf/beowulf.html

Excellent resource on *Beowulf*, featuring links to the original Old English version, translations, a search facility and pictures of the original manuscript.

Romanticism on the Net
http://users.ox.ac.uk/~scat0385/

A peer reviewed electronic journal devoted to romantic studies. The site also contains a list of links to other sites, making it an excellent gateway for romantic and gothic literature. Upcoming conferences and calls for papers are published and the site makes excellent use of the electronic medium by encouraging feedback via a forum where opinions on previously published articles can be found.

Literature Online
http://lion.chadwyck.co.uk/

Extraordinary resource featuring a library of over a quarter of a million texts, a writer in residence, discussion groups and links to other literary resources. While the database searches require a subscription – check with your college library to find out if your institution already subscribes, access to the writer in residence – masterclass discussion groups and poems of the week are free, as is access to a small example database of love poetry.

Anthology of Middle English Literature
http://www.luminarium.org/medlit/

Beautifully designed and illustrated Java augmented site featuring musically accompanied resources on Chaucer, Sir Gawain, William Langland, Julian of Norwich, William Kempe, Thomas Malory and Medieval plays and poetry. Resources include links to further resources in each category making this an indispensable resource for Middle English.

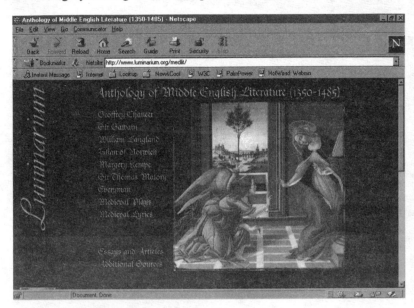

Figure 3.13 Luminarium

The Samuel Beckett Endpage

http://humanitas.ucsb.edu/projects/beckett/endpage.html

A well designed and comprehensive resource on Samuel Beckett, the highlight of which is an illustrated timeline which charts his life in meticulous detail. Also included are a short biography, a portrait gallery featuring stills from productions of his plays as well as pictures of the man himself, links to biographical texts, a Beckett Bulletin Board, a comprehensive list of publications by and about Beckett, calls for papers, links to other connected artists and authors and much more. This site caters as well for the casual browser as it does for the academic.

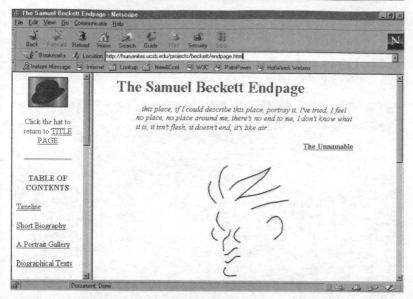

Figure 3.14 The Samuel Beckett Endpage

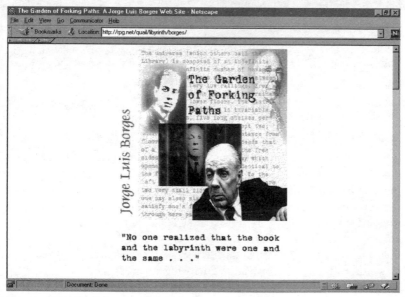

Figure 3.15 The Garden of Forking Paths

The Garden of Forking Paths
http://rpg.net/quail/libyrinth/borges/

This site is to Borges what Endpage is to Beckett, a sympathetically designed, comprehensive resource featuring links to biography, bibliography, selected quotations, drawings, papers, artists influenced by Borges and the intriguingly titled 'The Crimson Hexagon' – Books Borges Never Wrote.

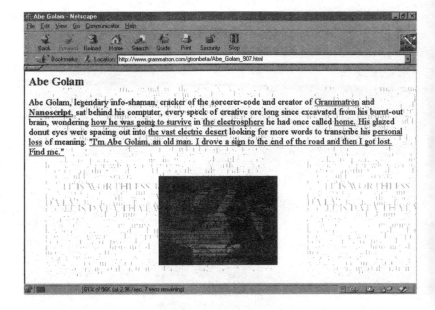

Figure 3.16 Mark Amerika's Grammatron

Grammatron
http://www.grammatron.com/

This is one of the most interesting examples of an electronic novel. It comes in two flavours; the high bandwidth version that drives itself through a series of screens with sound, animation and text forming a self-generating installation, and the low bandwidth version (illustrated) that is a more conventional hypertext, driven by the user. Both versions are well worth a visit.

4 | ART, ARCHITECTURE AND ARCHAEOLOGY

4.1 Aims of this chapter

This chapter aims to introduce the gateway resources in the areas of Fine Art, History of Art, Architecture and Archaeology. In addition, a number of sites worth browsing will be listed in the bookmarks sections.

4.2 Art

4.2.1 Art gateways

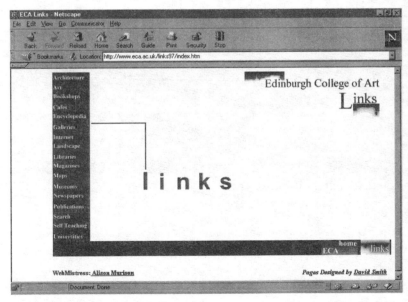

Figure 4.1 Edinburgh College of Art

Edinburgh College of Art Links
http://www.eca.ac.uk/links97/index.htm

Designed by David Smith, this is the best collection of art links of any Art School in the UK. The site is also very well designed, making imaginative and useful use of animation.

Rutgers Libraries Art Resources
http://www.libraries.rutgers.edu/rulib/artshum/art/art.html

Extensive collection of links to archives, libraries, museums, etc. Particularly good on art history and architecture.

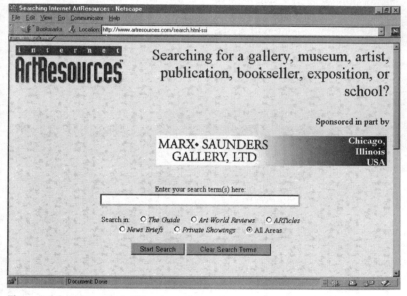

Figure 4.2 Internet ArtResources

Internet ArtResources
http://www.artresources.com/guide/

Describing itself as the largest searchable database of information on the visual arts, the guide has over 6,000 listings, with most areas showing images of work – currently, over 1,200 images are online. Particularly good on contemporary American art, listing galleries, publications, artists and art schools.

ADAM

http://adam.ac.uk/

Art, Design, Architecture and Media (ADAM) Information gateway, is a UK based site listing high quality resources for academia in the following categories:

- Fine Art, including paintings, prints and drawings, sculpture and other contemporary media and practices, including fine art using technology and performance art.
- Design, including industrial, product, fashion, graphic, packaging and interior design.
- Architecture, including town planning and landscape design, but excluding building construction.
- Applied Arts, including textiles, ceramics, glass, metals, jewellery and furniture.
- Media, including film, television, broadcasting, photography and animation.
- Theory; relevant historical, philosophical and contextual studies.
- Museum studies and conservation.
- Professional practice, related to any of the above.

ArtSource

http://www.uky.edu/Artsource/artsourcehome.html

The content of this gateway site is diverse and includes pointers to resources around the Internet as well as original materials submitted by librarians, artists and art historians etc. This site is intended to be selective, rather than comprehensive.

Voice of the Shuttle Art and Art History Page

http://humanitas.ucsb.edu/shuttle/art.html

Ignore at your peril – Voice of the Shuttle is perhaps the most comprehensive arts resource on the Internet, listing journals in addition to Web links.

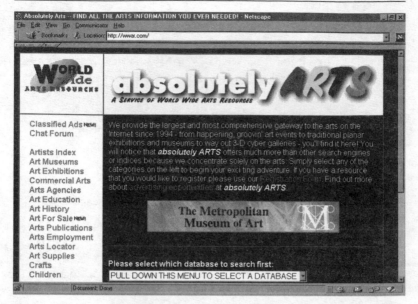

Figure 4.3 Absolutely Arts

Absolutely Arts World Wide Art Resources

http://wwar.com/

Claims with some justification to be the world's largest collection of art resources. Particularly useful for those considering a career in the arts, containing links to employment pages in addition to the thousands of research oriented links. The information on artists past and present is encyclopaedic in its scope and finely detailed.

The Web Museum, Paris

http://sunsite.doc.ic.ac.uk/wm/

Nicolas Pioch's Web Museum is a world wide network of art resources described by its creator as 'pleasureware'. Primarily a collection of art, the museum also contains biographical information on painters and a music section. The scope and quality of this project has to be experienced to be believed!

4.2.2 Art bookmarks

These first few bookmarks are self-explanatory, falling broadly into distinct periods in the history of art.

Russian Icons
http://www.auburn.edu/academic/liberal_arts/foreign/russian/icons/index.html

Italian Renaissance (1420–1600)
http://sunsite.doc.ic.ac.uk/wm/paint/tl/it-ren/

The Art of Renaissance Science: Galileo and Perspective
http://www.crs4.it/Ars/arshtml/arstitle.html

The First Impressionist Exhibition, 1874
http://www.artchive.com/74nadar.htm

Salvador Dali Virtual Museum of Art
http://www.nol.net/~nil/dali/gallery.html

Graphics intensive site devoted to the controversial surrealist.

Department of Objects and Delusions (Surrealist Imagery)
http://pharmdec.wustl.edu/juju/surr/images/surr-imagery.html

Fascinating collection of surrealist art. Organized by artist, each link containing lists of paintings which may be clicked to retrieve screen size renderings.

Perpetual Dada Surrealism
http://www.tc.umn.edu/~whit0580/igloo/

Richly illustrated site dedicated to the surrealists. Contains biographies, writings, pictures and more.

Mondrimat
http://www.stephen.com/mondrimat/

This site is essentially a 'Do it Yourself' Mondrian simulator, allowing the user to interactively adjust the blocks of colour until a 'Mondrian' is created.

4.3 Architecture

4.3.1 Architecture gateways

WWW Virtual Library – Architecture and Landscape Architecture
http://www.clr.toronto.edu:1080/VIRTUALLIB/arch.html

Exhaustive collection of links in a searchable database. As is usual at WWW Virtual Library sites, the listings include mailing lists, journals and conferences etc. in addition to the Web site listings.

Archihub
http://www.algonet.se/~archihub/index.html

Graphically intensive site, but worth the wait as the design quality is high. The resource lists are arranged in the following categories: General Resources, Countries, Competitions, 3D models, Marathon files, Newsgroups, Mailing lists, Recommended Destinations, Environmental, Urban Planning/Design, Image archives.

University of New South Wales: Architectural Web Sites
http://www.fbe.unsw.edu.au/misc/ArchSite/

Contains an excellent list of links under the 'Other Links of Interest' caption.

University of Nevada:Architecture Web Resources
http://www.nscee.edu/unlv/Libraries/arch/rsrce/webrsrce/

Vast collection of links, including newsgroups, journals and Web sites arranged alphabetically.

Lava Lab for Architecture
http://www.calibre.bwk.tue.nl/lava/links/

Small but perfectly formed collection of links to Web sites and architecture magazines.

Galaxy Architecture Page
http://galaxy.einet.net/galaxy/Humanities/Arts/Architecture.html

Aimed at the professional, this site contains links to academic sites, as well as public collections (including museums), directories and a search facility.

ArchWeb

http://cidoc.iuav.unive.it/architettura/archweb.ope/homenuova.html

Elegant listing from Andrea Visintini at the Istituto Universitario di Architettura di Venezia, available in English and Italian, links concerning architectural history are particularly good.

Death by Architecture Links

http://www.deathbyarch.com/html/general.html

Links to all things architectural, including journals, schools, organizations and (separately) English and non-English Web sites.

Cyburbia

http://www.arch.buffalo.edu/pairc/

Cyburbia (formerly called PAIRC – The Planning and Architecture Internet Resource Center) contains a comprehensive directory of internet resources relevant to planning, architecture, urbanism and other topics related to the built environment. Cyburbia also contains information about architecture and planning related mailing lists and Usenet newsgroups, and hosts several interactive message areas.

4.3.2 Architecture bookmarks

Great Buildings OnLine

http://www.greatbuildings.com/gbc/buildings.html

More than 750 great buildings from around the world and across history are listed below and illustrated at this Web site and The Great Buildings Collection CD-Rom, with photographic images, architectural drawings, discussion, bibliography, live 3D models and digital video clips.

ACADIA

http://acadia.org/

The Association for Computer Aided Design in Architecture, ACADIA was formed for the purpose of facilitating communication and information exchange regarding the use of computers in architecture, planning and building science. An organizer of conferences and publisher of the *ACADIA Quarterly*, a full listing of published papers is available on the resources page, though these are not available except through the printed medium.

Arcosanti – An Experimental City in Arizona
.http://www.arcosanti.org/

Paolo Soleri's experiment in fusing ecology with architecture.

...ellipsis... Contemporary and Avant-Garde Architecture
http://www.ellipsis.com/index.html

Featuring an innovative if opaque design, this site is well worth visiting for the catalogue of published work on architecture, as well as the sometimes tenuously assosciated links featured in the 'Things' and 'Other Things' sections.

QUONDAM Virtual Museum of Architecture
http://members.aol.com/quondam001/

Quondam was the first museum of architecture to exist solely in cyberspace, and virtuality defines the fundamental theme of Quondam's collection of 3-dimensional computer aided design (CAD) models, most of which represent unbuilt architectural designs.

The stated objective of Quondam and its collection is to manifest new virtual possibilities – enabling the user to 'visit' buildings that do not exist, to compare the scale of any number of buildings side by side, to analyse specific building designs by taking their 'models' apart and to learn by reassembling pieces of the 'models'.

Frank Lloyd Wright Source Page
http://www.mcs.com/~tgiesler/flw_home.htm

No architecture list could be complete without a Frank Lloyd Wright link. Of the many Web sites devoted to the work of this groundbreaking architect, this contains the most comprehensive collection of links and resources.

Modulor Man
http://home.earthlink.net/~lkuper/

A forum for the discussion of architecture, this site is especially notable for the pages devoted to these architects: Le Corbusier, Buckminster Fuller, Frank Gehry, Louis Kahn, Paul Lubowicki and Susan Lanier, Richard Meier, Gaetano Pesce, Bernard Tschumi and Frank Lloyd Wright, which are interesting studies of the people and their ideas.

Hans Netten's The High Rise Pages
http://www.xs4all.nl/~hnetten/

The High Rise Pages constitute an online high rise archive containing all
sorts of information, links and pictures of the tallest buildings, skyscrapers,
television towers, bridges, churches, monuments and other tall structures
from around the world.

4.4 Archaeology

4.4.1 Archaeology gateways

Voice of the Shuttle: Archaeology
http://humanitas.ucsb.edu/shuttle/archaeol.html

The definitive academic gateway resource, containing links to journals,
mailing lists and conferences as well as Web sites of interest.

Ancient World Web
http://www.julen.net/aw/

This Web site is a gateway to resources on all aspects of ancient history,
including cultural, culinary, economic, social, sexual and religious links.
Documents are accessible alphabetically via the meta index or directory
style through a subject specific index.

University of Waterloo Electronic Library Scholarly Resources Project – Archeology
http://www.lib.uwaterloo.ca/society/archaeol_soc.html

A collection of links to societies and associations, compiled specifically
on the basis of scholarly suitability.

Southampton Archaeology: Archaeological Links
http://avebury.arch.soton.ac.uk/NetStuff/archplaces.html

Links to journals, museums, organizations, other universities, VR models
and other archaeological indexes.

Archaeological Resource Guide for Europe (ARGE)
http://odur.let.rug.nl/arge/

ARGE represents the WWW Virtual Library for European Archaeology and is a comprehensive collection of links pointing to current archaeological communication and information resources including mailing lists, newsgroups and journals across Europe. These links can be accessed by country, by subject, by period, or by a database search.

4.4.2 Archeology bookmarks

The Celts and Saxons Homepage

http://www.primenet.com/~lconley/index.html

An excellent collection of links to sites with a Celtic or Saxon focus.

Sous les Mers – Underwater Archaeology

http://www.culture.fr/culture/archeosm.htm

French and English language pages, focusing on maritime archaeology, with richly illustrated details of wrecks and sites around the European coastlines and further afield.

Diotima – Women and Gender in the Ancient World

http://www.uky.edu/ArtsSciences/Classics/gender.html

Designed by Ross Scaife and Suzanne Bonefas, Diotima serves as an interdisciplinary resource for anyone interested in patterns of gender around the ancient Mediterranean. Diotima includes course materials, a searchable bibliography (with an emphasis on recent work), and links to many online articles, book reviews, databases and images.

Diotima also contains links to the essential Perseus database at Tufts University, (**http://www.perseus.tufts.edu**).

Bir Madhkur Excavations and Survey.

http://www.wam.umd.edu/~amsii/madhkur.htm

A detailed account of the Bir Madhkur excavations.

Guide to Resources for Study of the Ancient Near East

http://www-oi.uchicago.edu/OI/DEPT/RA/ABZU/ABZU.HTML

A project and publication of The Research Archives of the Oriental Institute, Chicago, compiled by Charles E. Jones, this is a comprehensive selection of resources, including links to maps, journals, library catalogues, museums and further links.

5 | BUSINESS, ENVIRONMENTAL AND SOCIAL SCIENCES

5.1 Aims of this chapter

This chapter aims to present a selection of resources that fall into the area covered by Business Studies, Environmental Studies and Social Sciences. These three categories represent areas that are currently well served with Internet based resources. Categories not listed explicitly here, may still be accessed through certain gateway sites – notably BUBL and the World Wide Web Virtual Library.

5.2 Business and Information Management

Business and Finance are areas that are increasingly well covered on the Internet. There are many business related resources that require subscription that are not listed here – these resources are intended for commercial purposes only and their inclusion is not appropriate in this context.

5.2.1 Business and Information Management gateways

Biz/ed

http://bized.ac.uk/

Biz/ed is an Internet service catering for the needs of students, teachers and lecturers working in the broad fields of economics and business. Supported by education and industry, Biz/ed draws on a wide range of expertise not only to point to quality educational sites but to host primary materials, most notably case studies, work sheets and substantial datasets not found elsewhere on the Internet. Notably, there is a policy decision not to include graphics, which means the site downloads faster than its competitors.

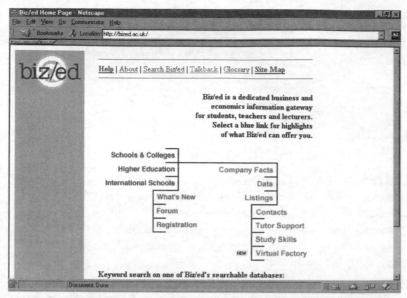

Figure 5.1 Biz/ed

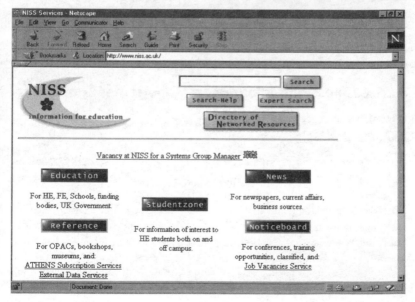

Figure 5.2 NISS

NISS

http://www.niss.ac.uk/

NISS (National Information Services and Systems) provides a gateway for education and research communities to access information resources worldwide, linking users to a wide range of services on the Internet. Like Biz/ed, NISS has a policy of keeping graphics to a minimum.

Ohio State University Virtual Finance Library

http://www.cob.ohio-state.edu/dept/fin/overview.htm

This is one of the most comprehensive gateway sites around, for all things financial. Separate and lengthy lists of links are provided for researchers, students and educators. There are also resource lists for investors, current market news and quotes.

Financial Information Link Library (FILL)

http://www.mbnet.mb.ca:80/~russell/

John Russell's FILL site is a Point Survey top 5% award winner, a gateway, pure and simple, the links are arranged by country.

WWW Virtual Library: Competitive Intelligence

http://crrm.univ-mrs.fr/vl/tech.html

Maintained by Dr Luc Quonium at CRRM, this branch of the WWW Virtual Library provides links to Gopher resources, the Competitive Intelligence Review and mailing lists, in addition to a large selection of associated Web sites.

WWW Virtual Library: Knowledge Management

http://www.brint.com/km/

Highly rated resource on knowledge management and intellectual capital.

WWW Virtual Library: Economics

http://netec.wustl.edu/WebEc/

http://netec.mcc.ac.uk/WebEc.html

WebEc describes itself as '... an effort to categorise free information in economics on the WWW. The original WebEc in Finland is mirrored in Japan, UK and USA. WebEc is awarded, framed and searchable and open

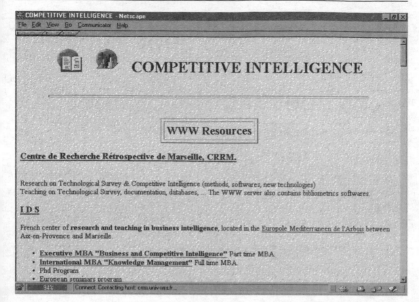

Figure 5.3 Competitive Intelligence

for additions and comments. It contains the List of Economics Journals. It is possible to read WebEc in different languages.'

5.2.2 Business and Information Management bookmarks

New York Stock Exchange

http://www.nyse.com/main.htm

Not as well resourced as the NASDAQ site, but interesting and easy to navigate.

Financial Times

http://www.usa.ft.com/

http://www.ft.com/

The Web site of the definitive financial newspaper, users must register, but this is free. Once registered the user can construct a portfolio of shares and monitor its progress on a day by day basis.

Strategy & Business
http://www.strategy-business.com/

Described as an extension to *Strategy & Business* magazine, this contains articles from the magazine, in addition to a library – lists of books on business, Web links and a forum where people can talk about business.

Money.Com
http://jcgi.pathfinder.com/money/plus/index.oft

Magazine format Web site, containing articles, polls etc. Aimed at the general market rather than the specialist business market.

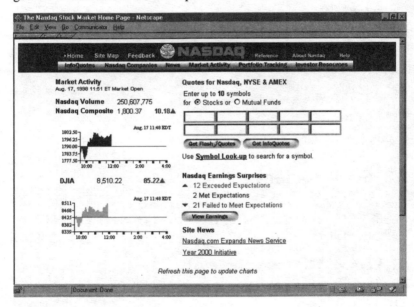

Figure 5.4 NASDAQ

NASDAQ
http://www.nasdaq.com/

As befits the Web site for the technology oriented stock market, this is a technically superb site, containing many resources including investor services, live graphics displaying the indexes and Java enabled portfolio tracking.

100 Rules for NASA Project Managers
http://pscinfo.pscni.nasa.gov/online/msfc/project_mgmt/100_Rules.html

Extraordinary collection of wisdom from NASA, for example:

> Rule #18: Most international meetings are held in English. This is
> a foreign language to most participants such as Americans, Germans,
> Italians, etc. It is important to have adequate discussions so that
> there are no misinterpretations of what is said.

The droll delivery of this collection does not detract from the quality of
the message.

The Economist
http://www.economist.com/

The Web site of the magazine. Features an article search facility with three
years' worth of archives.

Wall Street Journal
http://www.wsj.com/

Subscription required, but a two-week free trial makes it accessible.

5.3 Social Sciences

The Social Sciences present a large area that effectively crosses over into
a number of other areas, including humanities. This area is equally well
served by the Internet.

5.3.1 Social Science gateways

Social Science Information Gateway
http://sosig.ac.uk/

SOSIG is an online catalogue of thousands of high quality Internet resources
relevant to social science education and research. Every resource has been
selected and described by a librarian or subject specialist.

BIDS International Bibliography of the Social Sciences
http://www.bids.ac.uk/ibss.html

BIDS IBSS Online provides access to the International Bibliography of the Social Sciences, one of the largest and most comprehensive social science databases in the world. The database is supplied by the IBSS unit at the British Library of Political and Economic Science (BLPES). This database covers the core social science disciplines of Economics, Sociology, Politics and Anthropology.

Empowerment Resources

http://www.empowermentresources.com/

Describing itself as offering Tools For Personal Growth, Social Change, and Ecology, this site offers links to dozens of Web resources with a theme of personal, cultural and political empowerment.

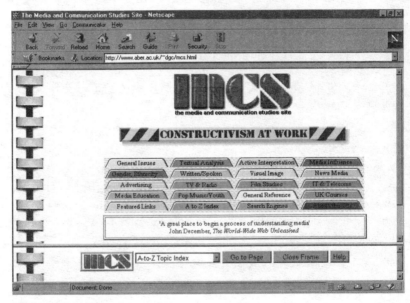

Figure 5.5 MCS

MCS

http://www.aber.ac.uk/~dgc/mcs.html

The MCS (pronounced 'mix') site is a British based gateway to Web resources useful in the academic study of media and communication. It was established in Spring 1995 and is being developed by Dr Daniel Chandler, lecturer in Media Theory at the Department of Education in the

University of Wales, Aberystwyth (UWA). It is the most comprehensive listing of quality resources available in the area of media studies, encountered in this survey.

SCOUT Report for Social Sciences

http://scout.cs.wisc.edu/scout/report/socsci/

The Scout Report for Social Sciences is aimed at students, librarians and lecturers in the social sciences. Each issue offers a selective collection of Internet resources covering topics in the field that have been chosen by librarians and academics working in the given area of study.

BOPCAS (British Official Publications Current Awareness Service)

http://www.soton.ac.uk/~bopcas/

You can use BOPCAS to browse lists of UK Parliamentary or Departmental publications indexed by date, publication type and policy area. BOPCAS also contains links to all UK government Web sites, and various policy awareness mailing lists.

CCTA Government Information Service

http://www.open.gov.uk/

As an interface to the government, this site could hardly be bettered; it indexes documents held on other UK government servers as well as its own server. This means that you may use the search facilities as the starting point for locating virtually any UK national and local government information published on the Web.

Institute for Research in Social Science Data Archive

http://www.irss.unc.edu/data_archive/

The IRSS Data Archive at the University of North Carolina is one of the oldest and largest archives of machine-readable data in the United States. It is the exclusive national repository for Louis Harris public opinion data. Other major sources of data include the Roper Center's International Survey Library Association (ISLA), which provides access to most non-proprietary public opinion data; the Inter-university Consortium for Political and Social Research (ICPSR), which stores and distributes data from both individual researchers and most federally funded social science studies; and the North

Carolina State Data Center, which distributes census data and the National Center for Health Statistics. IRSS also serves as the local repository for the World Fertility Surveys, and the Demographic and Health Surveys (DHS). Since 1991 it has been the repository for a large and growing number of state surveys, which it has made part of the National Network of State Polls archive.

OMNI (Organizing Medical Networked Information)
http://omni.ac.uk/

OMNI is a gateway to high quality Internet resources in medicine, biomedicine, allied health, health management and related topics. It aims to provide comprehensive coverage of the UK resources in this area and access to the best resources worldwide.

5.3.2 Social Science bookmarks

INCORE (Initiative on Conflict Resolution and Ethnicity at the University of Ulster)
http://www.incore.ulst.ac.uk/cds/countries/

These geographically grouped guides provide information about Internet resources on conflict and ethnicity specific to particular countries and regions.

MORI Research Centre
http://www.mori.com/

The Web site of the famous opinion pollsters, the details of many polls are accessible from this site.

The Center for the Study of Group Processes
http://www.uiowa.edu/~grpproc/

Home of *Current Research in Social Psychology* (an electronic journal), this site contains many links to other sites of interest.

HOMENET
http://homenet.andrew.cmu.edu/progress/

A study at Carnegie Mellon University into how people use the Internet.

Regent Online Journal of Communication

http://www.regent.edu/acad/schcom/rojc/rojc.html

A refereed online journal devoted to the discussion of communication theory.

Sociological Research OnLine

http://www.socresonline.org.uk/socresonline/

Sociological Research OnLine publishes high quality applied sociology, focusing on theoretical, empirical and methodological discussions which engage with current political, cultural and intellectual topics and debates.

The Durkheim Pages

http://eddie.cso.uiuc.edu/Durkheim/

These pages are devoted to the presentation of information concerning the great French sociologist and philosopher, Emile Durkheim (1858–1917). They have been prepared and are maintained by Robert Alun Jones, Professor of Religious Studies, History and Sociology at the University of

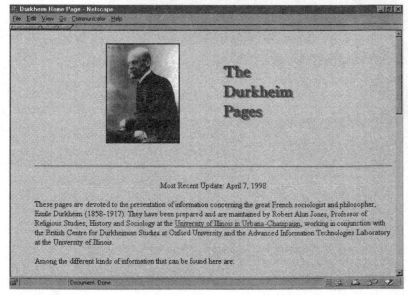

Figure 5.6 The Durkheim Pages

Illinois in Urbana-Champaign, working in conjunction with the British Centre for Durkheimian Studies at Oxford University and the Advanced Information Technologies Laboratory at the University of Illinois.

5.4 Environmental Studies

5.4.1 Environmental Studies gateways

BUBL Link: Environment
http://bubl.ac.uk/link/

High quality resource list from BUBL.

The Virtual Library on Urban Environmental Management
http://www.soc.titech.ac.jp/uem/

The UEM Homepage is an output of the Urban Environmental Management Research Initiative (UEMRI), a grouping of urban planning researchers from around the world. It looks at urban areas as the intersection of natural, built and socio-economic environments.

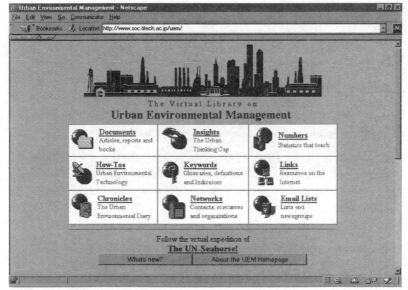

Figure 5.7 UEM

Amazing Environmental Organization Web Directory
http://www.webdirectory.com/

With thousands of sites, this is the largest exclusively environmental organization directory on the Web and includes sites from over 100 countries.

John Rylands University Library Manchester, Earth Sciences: Internet Resources
http://rylibweb.man.ac.uk/data1/ir/info/earthsci.html

Excellent and large collection of links in the area of Earth Sciences.

Cyburbia
http://www.arch.buffalo.edu/pairc/

Cyburbia (formerly called PAIRC – The Planning and Architecture Internet Resource Center) contains a comprehensive directory of Internet resources relevant to planning, architecture, urbanism and other topics related to the built environment. Cyburbia also contains information about architecture and planning related mailing lists and Usenet newsgroups, and hosts several interactive message areas.

Gaia Related Sites
http://www.mystical-www.co.uk/gaia1.htm

A large collection of links to both scientific and alternative resources.

5.4.2 Environmental Studies bookmarks

Biodiversity and Conservation
http://darwin.bio.uci.edu/~sustain/bio65/Titlpage.htm

A hypertext book by Peter J. Bryant, School of Biological Sciences, University of California. The book deals with the problems of trying to preserve biological diversity on the Earth. Topics include the history of life, depletion and extinction from over-exploitation, exotic introductions and deforestation.

European Forest Institute
http://www.efi.fi/

An independent non-governmental organization conducting European forest research.

Figure 5.8 Biodiversity and Conservation

Science and the Environment

http://www.ec.gc.ca/science/splash.htm

A valuable source of scientific information on the key environmental challenges facing Canadians.

European Tropical Forest Research Network

http://www.etfrn.org/etfrn/etfrn-home.html

The European Tropical Forest Research Network (ETFRN) aims to contribute to the international efforts towards wise, sustainable management and protection of (sub)tropical forests and woodlands. The Web site publishes data and information from projects involved in tropical and subtropical forest research.

Friends of the Earth

http://www.foe.org/

http://www.foe.co.uk/

Friends of the Earth is an environmental group, dedicated to preserving the planet from the ravages of industry. They have an international network over dozens of countries and have attracted wide ranging support for their activities.

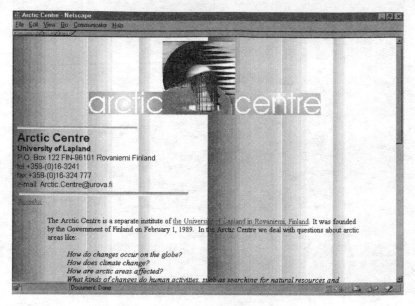

Figure 5.9 Arctic Centre

Arctic Centre – University of Lapland
http://www.urova.fi/~arktinen/

The Arctic Centre is a research institute attached to the University of Lapland, their activities include research into questions such as:

- 'What kinds of changes do human activities, such as searching for natural resources and extracting them, cause to nature in the Arctic?' and
- 'How do the indigenous peoples of arctic areas adapt to nature and changes in society?'

Department of the Environment (UK)
http://www.detr.gov.uk/

The official pages of the UK Department of the Environment, containing a wealth of links to all aspects of the government's environmental strategies.

6 SCIENCE

6.1 Aims of this chapter

This chapter will introduce the gateway sites for science resources on the Internet. Sciences represented in detail are Computer Science, Physics, Mathematics, Biology and Chemistry. A selection of science related sites are listed in the 'Bookmarks' section of each category.

Gateways that serve Science in all its guises are included here:

BUBL

http://bubl.ac.uk/link/subjects/

Although not strictly a dedicated science gateway, BUBL is very strong on science indexes, containing links to subject specific journals and societies, numerous pathways within a particular subject, and links to general resources, i.e. other gateway sites.

The A–Z List of Electronic Journals

http://www.lib.cam.ac.uk/InformationServices/journals.html

Self explanatory – a compendium of electronic journals – not exclusive to the Sciences.

6.2 Computer Science

6.2.1 Computing gateways

Guide to Computer Science Internet Resources

http://www.library.ucsb.edu/istl/97-summer/internet2.html

Michael Knee's Guide to Computer Science Internet Resources at the

University Library, University at Albany, is an excellent resource, containing links to resources in the areas of Algorithms, Associations, Bibliographies/Technical Reports, Dictionaries, Electronic Resources, Facts & Figures and Programming Languages, in addition to a list of gateway sites entitled 'Starting Points'.

World Internet Directory – Computer and Internet
http://www.tradenet.it/links/coin/coin.html

Notable for containing links to the FAQs of many newsgroups, in addition to a very extensive directory of links to Internet resources of all kinds – mainly useful for finding out about specific hardware and software as the links are arranged alphabetically under various categories and the site lacks a search facility.

ComputingSite – The Knowledge Search Engine
http://www.computingsite.com/

Somewhat confusingly, this is not a Computing specialist site, more of a directory with the subject areas arranged in 'channels'. The site does however sport a search engine.

The History of Computing
http://ei.cs.vt.edu/~history/

This collection of materials is provided courtesy of the Department of Computer Science at Virginia Tech, and is sponsored in part by a grant from the National Science Foundation.

Much more than a historical site, The History of Computing has sections devoted to the following topics of interest: Overviews of the History of Computing, People and Pioneers, Machines (including a special section on Cryptographic machines), Programming Languages, Calculators, Organisations and Museums, Archives and Collections, Publications, Networks and Internet, and Women in Computing History.

WWW Virtual Library: Computing
http://src.doc.ic.ac.uk/bySubject/Computing/Overview.html

The WWW Virtual Library Computing resources at Imperial College, London; it is hard to imagine that any quality computing resources have escaped the compilers of this site.

Yahoo: Computer Science

http://www.yahoo.co.uk/Science/Computer_Science/

Yahoo is amongst the largest directories available, and definitely worth browsing through – content is not strictly academic.

Virtual Computer Library

http://www.utexas.edu/computer/vcl/

The Virtual Computer Library is a collection of hundreds of links to information about computers and computing put together at the University of Texas.

Developer.com

http://www.developer.com/directories/

A peerless resource specializing in Internet applications, providing information in directories arranged in the following categories: ActiveX, ASP, C/C++, Cold Fusion, CGI, Databases, Distributed Objects, HTML/ DHTML, Intranets, Java, JavaScript, Middleware, Networks & Systems, Perl, Push Technology, Visual Basic, VRML, and XML.

W3 Consortium

http://www.w3.org/

The W3 Consortium is the organization that administers standards on the WWW. Their Web site is mandatory visiting if you are interested in what is going to be the state of the art next year. It also contains the source documentation for all versions of HTML, and news of the W3 journal and conferences.

6.2.2 Computing bookmarks

Charles Babbage Institute

http://www.cbi.umn.edu/

The Charles Babbage Institute of Computer History (CBI) is a research centre at the University of Minnesota dedicated to promoting the study and preservation of the history of information processing.

SiliconBase

http://www-leland.stanford.edu/group/itsp/

Part of The Information Technology and Society Project (ITSP) at Stanford

University, SiliconBase provides a forum where scholars, students, professionals and corporations explore the history, sociology, politics, economics and culture of the digital age.

Project Cool Developer Zone
http://www.projectcool.com/developer/

A site dedicated to Web site design, featuring tutorials for HTML and JavaScript. Searchable database of links, including mailing lists.

Web Monkey
http://www.hotwired.com/webmonkey/frontdoor/index.html

Another excellent how-to guide for Web developers, from *Wired* magazine.

JavaWorld
http://www.javaworld.com/javasoft.index.html

Magazine format site for serious Java developers; articles published each month include tutorial material as well as discussion of the technical aspects of the language and commentary on new technologies as they appear.

The ADA Project
http://www.cs.yale.edu/HTML/YALE/CS/HyPlans/tap/tap.html

Elisabeth Freeman and Susanne Hupfer's valuable resource for women in computing, links to journals and conferences, careers information in academia, organizations and discussion groups.

6.3 Chemistry

6.3.1 Chemistry gateways

BIDS RSC Databases
http://www.bids.ac.uk/rsc.html

The BIDS RSC service provides access to seven databases supplied by The Royal Society of Chemistry. These databases cover subject areas such as analytical chemistry, chemical engineering, health and safety, biotechnology, nutrition, mass spectrometry and news from the chemical and allied industries.

CHEMINFO
http://www.indiana.edu/~cheminfo/

This useful resource, compiled and maintained at Indiana University by Gary Wiggins, contains a number of categories, including Discussion List archives (searchable), and the Clearinghouse for Chemical Information Instructional Materials which contains items developed by librarians, chemists and commercial organizations to teach the use of chemical information sources.

ChemCenter
http://www.chemcenter.org/

Access conference announcements, journals and databases through this site, which focuses on professionals, educators and researchers.

Links for Chemists
http://www.liv.ac.uk/Chemistry/Links/links.html

This site at the University of Liverpool is a searchable index of over 3,750 Chemistry resources on the WWW.

6.3.2 Chemistry bookmarks

Center for Clouds, Chemistry and Climate
http://www-c4.ucsd.edu/

Research centre including details of their Indian Ocean experiment (INDOEX) on the influence of aerosols on global warming. The Center is a National Science Foundation Science and Technology Center, Scripps Institution of Oceanography, University of California, San Diego.

Chemistry Art Gallery
http://www.liv.ac.uk/Chemistry/ArtGallery.html

Famously fascinating gallery of images from the University of Liverpool.

The Electronic Nobel Museum Project
http://www.nobel.se/enm-index.html

Clicking on the Nobel Prize link loads a page from where the user can input subject headings – Chemistry for example – to retrieve a list of Nobel prize winners and details of their lives and prize winning activities.

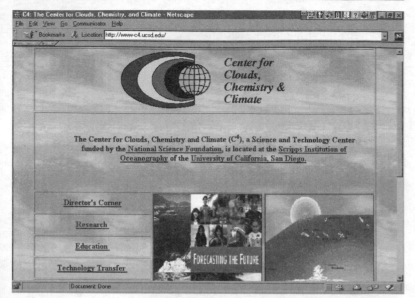

Figure 6.1 Center for Clouds, Chemistry and Climate

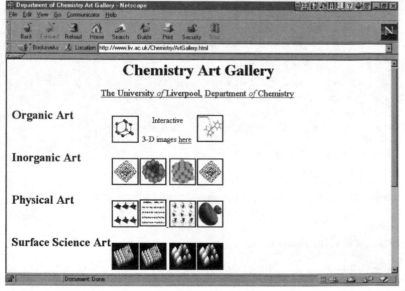

Figure 6.2 Chemistry Art Gallery

6.4 Physics

6.4.1 Physics gateways

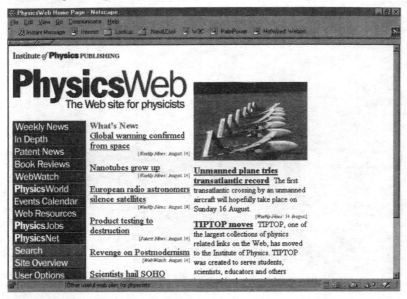

Figure 6.3 PhysicsWeb

PhysicsWeb

http://physicsweb.org/

Magazine style Web site for physicists, containing articles, links and news.

Institute of Physics

http://www.iop.org/

Links to journals, magazines and bibliographies, and TIPTOP (The Internet Pilot to Physics) which is a resource containing a vast collection of links to Physics related sites, the Virtual Laboratory containing Java, VRML and Shockwave visualisations and the Physics forum containing conference announcements, book reviews and a student forum.

WWW Virtual Library: Physics

http://www.fisk.edu/vl/Physics/Overview.html

A gateway to specialized areas of Physics, Physics departments around the world and electronically published papers.

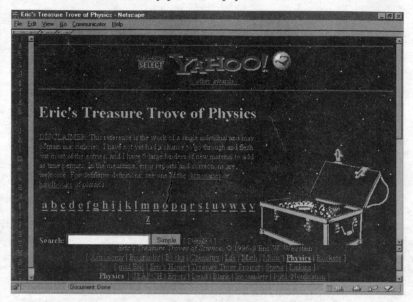

Figure 6.4 Eric's Treasure Trove of Physics

Eric's Treasure Trove of Physics

http://www.astro.virginia.edu/~eww6n/physics/physics.html

This is part of a much larger site dedicated to science. An encyclopaedia of terms and definitions, accessible alphabetically or via the on-site search engine. Also features chapters dedicated to Mathematics, Music, Astronomy, Rocketry and Chemistry. Remarkably this resource is all the work of one person – Dr Eric W. Weisstein of the Astronomy Department at the University of Virginia.

6.4.2 Physics bookmarks

Albert Einstein Online

http://www.westegg.com/einstein/

Copiously resourced site on Albert Einstein, contains writings, including the Relativity Texts and links to other Web based resources.

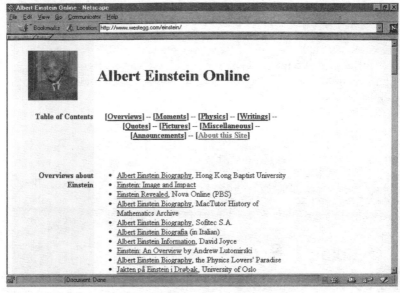

Figure 6.5 Albert Einstein Online

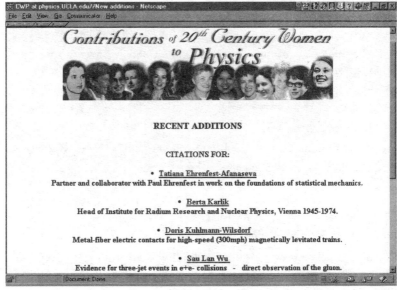

Figure 6.6 Contributions of 20th Century Women to Physics

Contributions of 20th Century Women to Physics

http://www.physics.ucla.edu/~cwp/

Presented here are citations of twentieth century women who have made original and important contributions to physics. The citations describe briefly, and document, selected major scientific contributions. They also contain biographical information – mainly pertaining to the scientific lives of the women.

The Laws List

http://www.alcyone.com/max/physics/laws/

Alphabetical index to laws, rules, principles, effects, paradoxes, limits, constants, experiments and thought-experiments in physics, compiled by Erik Max Francis.

6.5 Biology

6.5.1 Biology gateways

Biodiversity and Biological Collections Web Server

http://biodiversity.uno.edu/

This WWW server is devoted to information of interest to systematists and other biologists of the organismic kind. Contains links to specimens in biological collections, taxonomic authority files, directories of biologists, an archive of the Taxacom, MUSE-L and CICHLID-L listservs, and access to online journals.

Mann Library Gateway

http://www.mannlib.cornell.edu/cgi-bin/subj.cgi?subject=Biology

Cornell University's computer generated index to Biology related resources.

OMNI Subject Listing for Biology

http://roads.omni.ac.uk/listings/QH1.html

Alphabetical listing of resources including newsgroups, mailing lists, biology departments and Web based resources such as the Online Biology Book.

Biology on the Internet: Selected sites
http://www.iat.unc.edu/guides/irg-14.html

Very extensive collection of specialist biology resources compiled by: Carolyn Kotlas and Debra Hanken at the Institute for Academic Technology.

6.5.2 Biology bookmarks

Online Biology Book

http://gened.emc.maricopa.edu/bio/bio181/BIOBK/BioBookTOC.html

Quite literally, this resource is an online biology book by M.J. Farabee. Based on lecture notes and compiled over a number of years, this is a useful resource for biology students.

6.6 Mathematics

6.6.1 Mathematics gateways

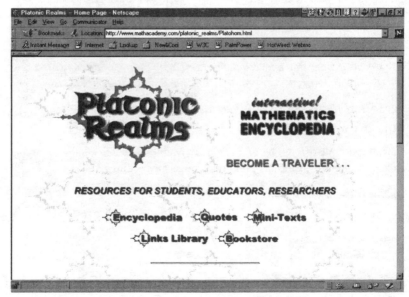

Figure 6.7 Platonic Realms ©

Platonic Realms ©

http://www.mathacademy.com/platonic_realms/Platohom.html

Good selection of resources for students, lecturers and researchers.

Herriot-Watt Mathematics Home Page

http://www.ma.hw.ac.uk/maths_extern.html

Small but none the less useful selection of Maths resources.

MathSearch

http://www.maths.usyd.edu.au:8000/MathSearch.html

A collection of over 140,000 documents on English language mathematics and statistics servers across the Web – most of the material here is at university and research level.

WWW Virtual Library: Mathematics

http://euclid.math.fsu.edu/Science/math.html

Divides its resources into the following categories: Addresses, Bibliographies, Department Web Servers, Education, Electronic Journals, General Resources, Gophers, High School Servers, Newsgroups, Preprints, Science and Math, Software, Specialized Fields, and TeX Archives*.

*TeX is a software that enables the writing and reading of documents using the extended character set required for mathematical symbols.

European Mathematical Information Service

http://www.EMIS.DE/

Part of a service offered by the European Mathematical Society – contains links to databases, journals and conference proceedings.

Mathematics Archives Web Server

gopher://archives.math.utk.edu:80/hGET%20/index.html

Web links, searchable database, proceedings of conferences, teaching materials and software are all accessible here.

BUBL Link: Mathematics

http://link.bubl.ac.uk/mathematics/

Mailing lists, journals, societies, software and preprints are accessible from here, in addition to the selections of generalized and specialized links.

6.6.2 Mathematics bookmarks

The MacTutor History of Mathematics Archive
http://www-groups.dcs.st-and.ac.uk/~history/

The History of Mathematics archive is part of the Mathematical MacTutor system developed at the School of Mathematical and Computational Sciences University of St Andrews for learning and experimenting with mathematics.

The archive contains the biographies of more than 1,100 mathematicians plus articles on the development of mathematical ideas cross-referenced to the biographies. There is a collection of more than 60 articles on Famous Curves which have been extensively studied by mathematicians, giving their history as well as pictures of the curves and various curves (evolutes, inverses, caustics etc.) which are associated with them. If your browser is capable of handling Java, you have the option of experimenting with these curves in an interactive way.

e-Math
http://e-math.ams.org/

The American Society of Mathematics Web site contains details of its own journals and conferences. In addition there are some useful research resources listed under 'Publications and Research Tools' including MathSciNet, a searchable Web database covering over 50 years of mathematical publications.

The Galileo Project
http://es.rice.edu/ES/humsoc/Galileo/

The Galileo Project at Rice University is a hypertext source of information on the life and work of Galileo Galilei (1564–1642) and the science of his time.

The Most Common Errors in Undergraduate Mathematics
http://math.vanderbilt.edu/~schectex/commerrs/

A cry from the heart – 'I am tired of seeing these same old errors over and over again. (I would rather see new, original errors!)'!

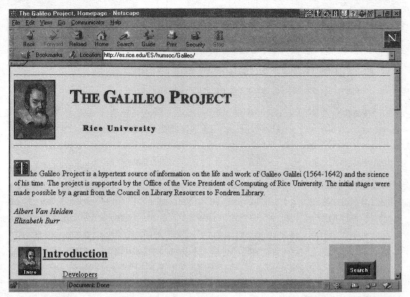

Figure 6.8 The Galileo Project

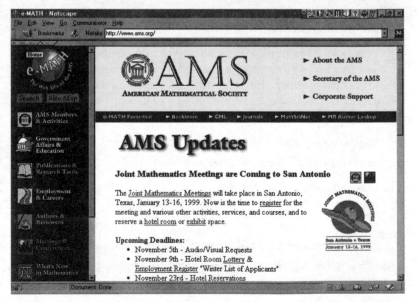

Figure 6.9 The American Mathematical Society, home to E-math

The Alan Turing Internet Scrapbook

http://www.turing.org.uk/turing/scrapbook/

Maintained by Andrew Hodges, author of 'Breaking the Code', these pages provide a fascinating insight into the work of Alan Turing.

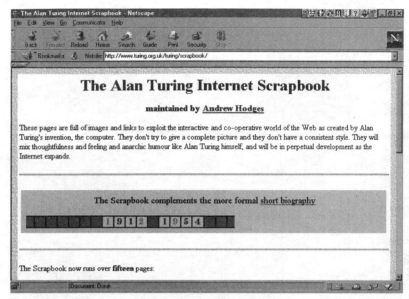

Figure 6.10 The Alan Turing Internet Scrapbook

History of Mathematics

http://aleph0.clarku.edu/~djoyce/mathhist/mathhist.html

Mainly concerned with the history of mathematics, but also carries a list of useful mathematically oriented links.

Grace Hopper

http://www.cs.yale.edu/HTML/YALE/CS/HyPlans/tap/Files/hopper-story.html

Biography of one of the pioneers of early computer programming.

John von Neumann
http://ei.cs.vt.edu/~history/VonNeumann.html

Biography of von Neumann the mathematician, and promoter of the stored program concept used in computer architectures.

Part Three

GETTING THE BEST OUT OF THE INTERNET

In this part of the book, we will see how the Internet can be used as a resource to improve both work and leisure.

In Chapter 7 – The Web as an Entertainment Resource – we examine the resources available in support of leisure activities including sport, cooking, music and going out.

In Chapter 8 – Using the Web as a Research Resource – we see how the Web can be used to perform productive academic research quickly. This part is illustrated by two case studies, one from Computer Science and one from Humanities. This chapter will also deal with the correct way to credit material gleaned from the Web.

7 | THE WEB AS AN ENTERTAINMENT RESOURCE

7.1 Aims of this chapter

Whether you are staying in, or going out, this chapter shows how you can use the Web to enhance your quality time.

7.2 Sport

These listings should appeal as much to the armchair fan as the practitioner. Even if you are stuck in the library on a rainy Saturday afternoon and you need to find out the latest score in the cup final ... read on!

7.2.1 Soccer

Soccernet

http://www.soccernet.com/

Focusing on the English Premier League, giving live score updates and a SoccerFlash news feature, this site also contains information and news about European and global soccer.

CarlingNet

http://www.fa-premier.com/

The official English Premier League Web Site, links to all the clubs and match reports.

Irish Football Site

http://www.clubi.ie/fpage/

The official Irish football site.

MLSNet – Major League Soccer
http://www.mlsnet.com/

The official US Major League Soccer site.

J.League Home Page
http://www.j-league.or.jp/index.html

The official Japanese J.League soccer site.

Italian Serie A
http://www.finalwhistle.com/euro/italyindex.html

An unofficial, but no less comprehensive site devoted to Italian football in all its glory.

7.2.2 American football

Super Bowl Summaries
http://www.cs.ucr.edu/~entezari/SuperBowl.html

Billed as the ultimate NFL Page, this is an extensive resource, with links to latest odds, news, scores, standings etc. plus a downloads page for football screen savers and a host of non-football related items such as 'Cool Java Code'!

NFL Super Bowl Archives
http://home.earthlink.net/~ob1gui/nflsbar/nflsbarc.htm

This page compiles complete scores and schedules from 1966 (Super Bowl I) to the present year. What's unique about this site is that it uses a computer ranking system than can be used to compare teams from different years regardless of the number of games played or differences in the playoff systems over the years!

7.2.3 Cricket

Lord's – The Home of Cricket
http://lords.msn.com/news/headlines/default.htm

Nicely designed site, brings news, scores, team details and historical archives to the desktop.

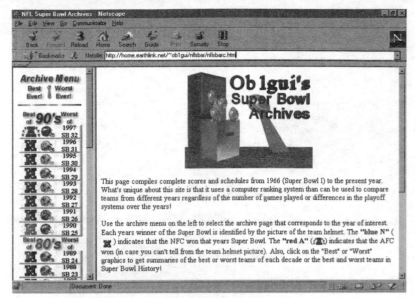

Figure 7.1 Ob1gui's Super Bowl Archives

Sky Sports Cricket Home Page

http://www.skysports.co.uk/sports/cricket/

International and league cricket are covered in this well organized site which brings the latest news as it happens – almost.

7.2.4 Baseball

Major League Baseball

http://www.majorleaguebaseball.com/

This is the official site of MLB in America and it presents news, photos, highlights, scoreboard and the clubhouse shop.

ESPN SportsZone: Major League Baseball

http://espn.sportszone.com/mlb/

Sports magazine format, bringing news, club details and a chat forum.

7.2.5 Tennis

ATP Tour Official Site

http://www.atptour.com/en/

Listings of tournaments, results and players from the ATP circuit.

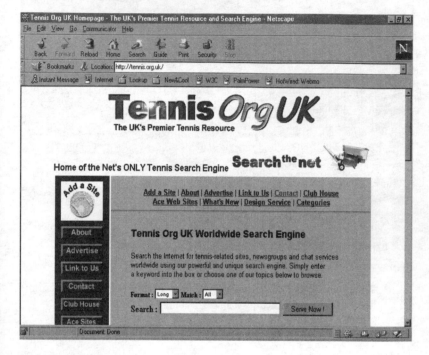

Figure 7.2 Tennis Org UK

Tennis Org UK

http://tennis.org.uk/

Home of the world's only tennis search engine, this excellent site also contains information about health, technique, the players, tournaments (Grand Slam, ATP, WTA and ITF) and tennis associations as well as links to other tennis sites and lists of equipment shops. Pretty much everything you could wish for in a sports site!

7.3 Food

7.3.1 Recipes

Can't cook? won't cook? – there's no longer any excuse – these Web sites purvey recipes from the cheap and cheerful to the frankly gluttonous. Gastronomer and Meals.Com go the extra mile with features that are aimed at the beginner, such as automatic shopping list creation based on your recipes (Meals.Com).

Yahoo Directory: Cooking

http://www.yahoo.com/Society_and_Culture/Food_and_Drink/Cooking/

The Yahoo directory lists virtually every site which has anything to do with food, from diets to drinking games, it's all here.

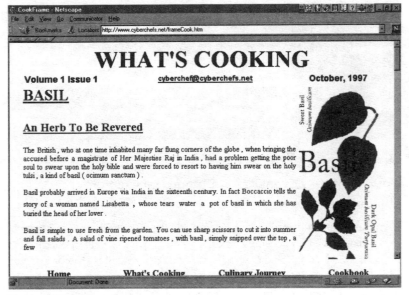

Figure 7.3 Cyberchef

Cyberchef

http://www.cyberchefs.net/

Recipes, articles, chef profiles and links.

The Internet Chef

http://www.ichef.com/

This is the best food site surveyed; with dozens of featured recipes, a vegetarian section, bulletin board for posting recipes – literally hundreds of recipes posted here. Articles, tips – this site is a must!

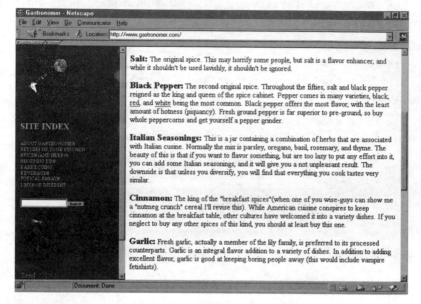

Figure 7.4 Gastronomer

Gastronomer – Adventures in Culinary Excellence

http://www.gastronomer.com/

If you suffer from fear of cooking, this is the site that will turn the beginner into a decent cook in no time – articles explain every aspect of cooking, as if addressing a complete beginner with lots of promise! – How to prepare a kitchen, How to Shop, What are Herbs and Spices for, the Art of Barbecue. The site is obviously composed by someone who really loves their food.

Meals.com – All things Cooking

http://www.meals.com/index.html

Meals.com gives you more than just recipes. Extras include seasonal and non-seasonal menu suggestions in the Recipe Center section; chat rooms where you can compare notes with other chefs; a Meal Planning Calendar where you can plan up to a week's worth of meals; and most usefully, an editable Custom Shopping List that includes all the ingredients from all the recipes you select.

7.4 Music

Budget is always a consideration of the music lover, and if your budget stretches to it, for the UK purchaser it can work out cheaper to purchase CDs in quantities of three or more, from the US and have them sent by courier. This is because CDs in the UK are more expensive than anywhere else in the world. Typically a CD bought in a high street store in London will cost between £12 and £15, whereas in New York for example, the same CD will cost between $12 and $15 which amounts to almost 50% off the price. Many stores in New York do mail order via e-mail, and with the additional cost of a courier (approximately the cost of an extra CD at American prices) you can buy three CDs there, for the price of two in the UK! (Remember, you will be required by Customs and Excise to pay VAT.)

The following listings provide gateway sites for different types of music. Included in these listings are usually the e-mail address of various favoured record shops for specialist music.

7.4.1 Classical

The Classical Music site
http://musik.freepage.de/hlz/

The best feature of this site is the grading of budget classical recordings. There is a downloadable version of the ZET Music CD guide which lists over 7,000 classical recordings and the novel feature of a 'start up' collection for those who do not actually own any classical music.

Classical Music on the Web
http://www.edu.coventry.ac.uk/music/music.htm

Many pages of music links, featuring composer profiles, lists of works etc. Focuses on British Composers.

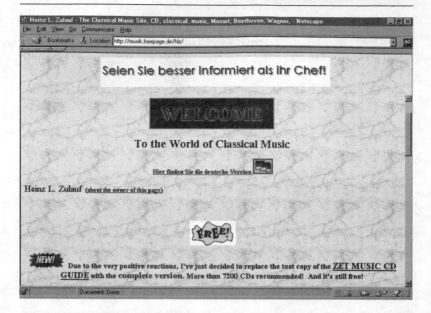

Figure 7.5 The Classical Music Site

Classical Net

http://www.classical.net/

A comprehensive gateway site, Classical Net provides a point-of-entry into a wide array of informational files about classical music – over 3,400 files at Classical Net and over 2,400 links to other classical music Web sites. Enjoy!

The Classical Music Email List Directory

http://www.netaxs.com/~jgreshes/lists/cd.html

This site catalogues every known mailing list that has anything to do with classical music. It provides a description of the list's purpose and detailed joining instructions. A superb resource for musicians and hobbyists alike.

7.4.2 Alternative

DIY Search

http://www.diysearch.com/

Figure 7.6 DIY Search

The gateway to all things alternative – humor, e-zines, art, literature, comics and of course, music. Great design and a searchable index.

IndieNet

http://www.geocities.com/SunsetStrip/Studio/7078/

Mission statement: 'To aid and foster growth in the independent music community by providing resources to bands, labels, fans, and more.'

Indie Music Resources

http://kathoderay.org/music/

A gateway site to the world of indie music.

The Music Note

http://www.musicnote.com/

This site offers Real Audio, enabling interested viewers and hopefully, record companies to listen to independently produced music.

Figure 7.7 The Music Note

Upend's Independent Artists' Services

http://www.idiom.com/~upend/ias/index.html

A Web site by artists, for artists. This is US-centric, but there is a lot of useful information about getting gigs, promoting yourself etc. that maps easily on to any other country with an indie music scene.

Grunnen Rocks

http://iglo.cpedu.rug.nl/~evert/grunnen.htm

A labour of love – this encyclopaedic site takes its definition of indie very seriously indeed. There are pages with links to clubs and record stores in Holland, but these are expanding to include other cities and other countries.

This site will either implode or expand to become the definitive indie document. Watch this space!

7.4.3 Jazz

Phone Soft Cyber-World: Jazz Links

http://www.phone-soft.com/cyber-world/0154.htm

A gateway to more jazz related sites than it is possible to visit in one lifetime!

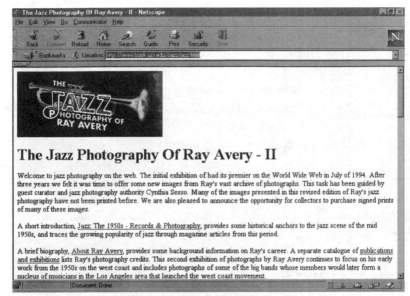

Figure 7.8 The Jazz Photography of Ray Avery

The Jazz Photography of Ray Avery - II

http://www.book.uci.edu/Jazz/jazz.html

Absolutely marvellous site, exhibiting atmospheric photographs of all the jazz greats – Miles Davis, Art Pepper, Chet Baker – the list goes on. This is the site's second incarnation; it now includes biographies and discographies, a bookstore and an opportunity to buy prints from the exhibition online.

Jazz Clubs Around the World

http://www.acns.nwu.edu/jazz/lists/clubs.html

Mostly focused on the US, but clubs in France, Austria, Gemany and Israel are also listed.

WNUR FM JazzWeb

http://www.acns.nwu.edu/jazz/

Divides its extensive resources into the following categories:
- Styles of Jazz (hypermap and essays)
- Artists (biographies, discographies, reviews)
- Performance (festivals, venues, reviews, regional jazz information)
- Jazz instruments (a revised approach)
- Media (radio, television, press)
- Jazz art
- Jazz education and musicianship
- Jazz retailers on the Internet
- Jazz labels on the Internet
- Other jazz resources on the Internet

An extraordinary project, the JazzWeb is a user-built volunteer project. The end goal of the JazzWeb is to contribute to the fantasy of finding all answers to all questions on demand. Resources are thoroughly compiled to the extent that certain artists' pages even feature the address of their mailing lists.

7.5 Going out

It is becoming increasingly easy to organise your time using Internet based resources. Many cities have districts which support their own Web sites, listing restaurants, shops etc.

On a global scale, *Time Out* does an excellent job of listings for a number of cities, and the Open World City Guide provides an excellent resource for travellers, which is no less useful if you are travelling from within the same country, including details of transport, and selected events.

Time Out

http://www.timeout.co.uk:81/

Site originating from the London based listings magazine covering film, theatre, sport, clubs, live music etc. Now expanded to include the following major cities: Amsterdam, Barcelona, Berlin, Boston, Brussels, Budapest,

Chicago, Dublin, Edinburgh, Glasgow, Las Vegas, London, Los Angeles, Madrid, Miami, New York, Paris, Philadelphia, Prague, Rome, San Francisco, Sydney, Tokyo and Washington, DC.

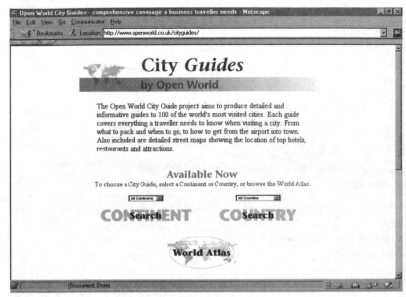

Figure 7.9 Open World City Guides

Open World City Guides

http://www.openworld.co.uk/cityguides/

Aimed at the business traveller, but no less useful for that, the cities included currently are: Amsterdam, Bali, Bath, Berlin, Boston, Cairo, Cape Town, Charleston, Edinburgh, London, New York, Paris, Shanghai, Singapore, Sydney, Tokyo, Vienna and Washington, DC.

Promising to appear soon are: Beirut, Lebanon; Rio de Janeiro, Brazil; Mexico City, Mexico; Hong Kong, China; Prague, Czech Republic; and Barcelona, Spain.

Each city has its own page, with links leading to information in the following categories: Passports and Visas; Electricity; Climate; Health; Getting there by boat, air, rail, bus, road and getting from the airport into town; Opening hours; Food and drink; Safety information; Photography;

Telephoning from (city); Around the (country in which city is found); Money matters – currency, exchange restrictions, credit cards, tipping, ATM information; Getting around town by road, bus, rail, boat, foot, taxi; Tourist information offices; Local climate; Geographical information; Images of (city); History; City centre maps; Accommodation; Attractions; Dining; Museums and galleries; Festivals and events; and Shops.

Student Travel Insurance

http://www.studentinsurance.co.uk

This site allows students to arrange property and travel insurance online, using credit card payments. The rates are apparently lower when purchased online.

7.6 Summary

Used as an information source, the Web can save you both money and time. The resources listed here are but the tip of the iceberg; there is no space to list all the raves, clubs and one-off festivals that are accessible via the Internet. As someone once said – seek and ye shall find!

One word of caution – where money is concerned, always check that the site is bona fide. In the case of record shops for example, it should be easy to find their address via a city guide or telephone directory. Always check before you part with money, and unless the shop has a secure transaction facility, do not send your credit card number over the Internet. Statistically, it is unlikely that this would result in a fraud, but why take the risk?

8 | USING THE WEB AS A RESEARCH RESOURCE

8.1 Aims of this chapter

In this chapter we will see how we can use the Web as a further research resource. Case studies from Computer Science and Humanities are provided, in which we will see how to get the best out of the search facilities available. We will see how documents quoted from the Web should be referenced, and why they should be referenced.

8.2 Library search vs. the Internet

Most projects, regardless of subject will involve a library search to begin with. This library search is supposed to be an information gathering exercise, and if done properly can provide you with a clear picture of the state of the art in any field.

There are four main types of information we might profitably look for on the Internet.

1 Research papers (all subject areas)
2 Industry 'white papers' (science)
3 Magazine articles (all subject areas)
4 Specialist academic Web sites within the subject area.

The first type, research papers are traditionally found in either conference proceedings or refereed journals. These represent the best of the research that is taking place in the academic community and some of the research in the commercial sector.

The second type, industry 'white papers' represent the definitive release to the public from an enterprise that has pioneered a technology or a methodology and wishes to make public some of the details.

Magazine articles can be found in paper form in most libraries, but the publisher's Web site will probably be equipped with a search engine which will make the search quick and easy.

The fourth category, specialist academic Web sites, contains sites such as Voice of the Shuttle, HUMBL, which serve as links to resources in certain subject areas (see Part Two, The Internet Resources).

Most subjects have their own governing body or society and that would be a good place to look for links towards specialised information. For example, a mandatory port of call for a computing assignment should be the British Computer Society Web site, which contains links to many areas of specialist interest, such as HCI (Human Computer Interaction), Artificial Intelligence and Programming Languages.

When searching for research material on the Web, remember that there is a great deal of poor material available. Generally speaking, if the author is affiliated with a university or professional body, such as the British Computer Society or if the paper is taken from a refereed journal or conference proceedings then the material should be reliable. Don't believe everything you read – wherever possible try to find more than one Web site, to give you a different perspective.

The research process can be split into the folowing stages:

General Research for up-to-date information

Sources include industry specific Web sites (for the sciences), online magazines and specialist magazine Web sites. Once a picture of the state of the art has been formed, we need to see if it builds upon any previous academic work.

Specific research for papers

This stage should begin with searches through the major gateway sites such as the WWW Virtual Library and BUBL Link. Once a number of sources have been acquired, we move on to the subject specific gateways, and through these, to journals and conference proceedings where available.

Is your thesis supported by the research findings?

Any academic project needs to be based on existing ideas, even if it contradicts these ideas. If the picture that has been formed from the first stage cannot be mapped on to the resources available from the second stage, one of two things has happened – either you have come up with a completely new idea (unlikely but not impossible) or your original impression is wrong. If the second condition applies, you need to re-read the generalized information to make sure that your impression is correct. If it is then you need to search more carefully for material on which you can base an argument.

Sorting the wheat from the chaff

The fruits of your research will fall into two categories. Papers that are useful in that they add to your understanding of an area and papers that are pivotal to your argument. It is up to you to decide which is which. The pivotal papers will often crop up as references in other papers. However, in the sense of being pivotal to your work, you need to find passages that can be cited. These passages should either confirm or contradict your thesis. Such papers form the basis of a successful project.

8.3 Case Study: Computer Science

More speed, less haste?

This assignment is aimed at first or second year computing students. Students compare the benefits of two technologies that are aimed at improving the speed of data communications over large Internetworks. These technologies are called Fast IP, created by Cisco Systems; and Tag Switching created by 3Com. Both of these have been featured in computer magazines such as *Byte*, *Computer Weekly* and *Computing* in the last twelve months and both are manufactured by large American companies. Our first decision is whether to look for the magazine articles or try to find the companies' Web sites.

Magazines will often give a less biased view than commerce, but magazines tend to rely on advertising for their existence and can be reluctant to alienate potential or existing clients by criticising their products. Magazines often include only a selection of articles on a Web site, as a trailer for a CD-Rom. For these reasons, a first step should be to look at the Web pages of each company, Cisco Systems and 3Com.

Finding the companies' Web sites is simple. As we discussed in Chapter 1, section 1.6, domain naming conventions in the USA suggest that the address of 3Com is **www.3Com.com** and **www.Cisco.com** should identify the Cisco Systems Web site. This principle works for most well known companies in the US, The English equivalent is to add **.co.uk** instead of **.com** to the company name.

Once there, we can see if these companies have their own search engines. Fortunately they do – it is generally the case that any major organisation will make some search tool available for visitors to the Web site. At this stage, it should simply be a matter of inputting the search terms in the appropriate form and waiting to see how much information is available.

The 3Com Web site's appropriate pages can be found by searching for the phrase FastIP. Interestingly this search also throws up pages from 3Com concerning Tag Switching, so there are already comparisons being made, though since these come from one of the competing companies we must be aware that it will not yield the full story. Having noted this reference, we can move on to the Web site's internal search engine and hunt for FastIP references. This yields 241 pages, many of which are translations into various languages. The search does deliver us the original white paper on the subject, which is the obvious place to begin reading. This search takes under five minutes.

It could be argued that searching for the search term + the name of the company on a search engine such as AltaVista would yield the same result. AltaVista will produce every reference from a world wide search. We would then have to filter the results to get to the pages we want. This would waste a great deal of time. At any point in time, thousands of people are probably using the well known search engines, so they can be very slow to return results. The rule of thumb is that if you can make life easier for the network, or the computer, do so. To illustrate this point we will look for Cisco Systems via AltaVista.

Searching for the word Cisco in AltaVista yields 33,124 hits. Obviously we will need to refine the search a little – the phrase 'Cisco Systems' + 'IP Switch' comes up with several hundred pages, one of which is a reference to IP Switching on the Cisco Web site. From here it is a simple matter to navigate towards the real information, by using the onsite search facility. This yields 82 texts with some reference to IP Switching. The entire search takes approximately ten minutes.

The next phase is to sort out the useful references. This process is exactly the same in principle as the library search. There is no short cut for reading the texts! One hint though is that a quick look at the document onscreen will often reveal whether it is likely to be useful or not. The useful ones can be bookmarked under a suitable heading, with the intention of retrieving them later for intensive reading; or saved to disk. Marginal or possibly useful papers can be bookmarked under a separate heading. Finally, the useful papers can be printed out for the serious business of annotation, references may be extracted and the research phase of the exercise is complete. This particular exercise yielded one white paper from 3Com and two papers from Cisco Systems, one of which contained an account of the technology in the wider context of internetworking.

After extracting the references from this material and making notes for the assignment, we can step back a little. We have got to the detailed material concerning these particular solutions; what we need now is some contextual material.

There may be other technologies worth mentioning, and there may be research underway that will produce better, faster technologies. For this type of material we need to look at research based institutions such as universities, and global communications companies such as British Telecom. Material gleaned from universities will be reliable, but in computing may not reflect the state of the art in practice. A multinational corporation such as BT has far greater resources than any university and will be better equipped. Such organisations also publish research papers from conferences and journals on the Web, which makes this type of resource very valuable to the researcher.

Having now searched the Web sites of the originating companies, and found some contextual material from other sources, all that remains is to check the appropriate magazine sites to track down any articles that may have been published over the last twelve months. The three sites I have chosen are *Byte* (USA), *Computer Weekly* (UK) and *Computing* (UK) magazines. Very little occurs in the computing industry without one or all of these magazines running an article on it.

Once the magazine search has been done, three useful articles have been located. This concludes the use of the Internet to enhance the research phase of this project. It is worth noting that because of the 'state of the art' nature of this project, the Internet can actually prove more fruitful than a conventional library search. This is unlikely to be the case with non-science disciplines, as use of the Internet has been slower to catch on in the research community for humanities subjects.

Articles and papers harvested from the Internet, must always be referenced correctly, just as if they were taken from a journal or library.

8.4 Case Study: Humanities

Living in the Digital Age: science fact or science fiction?

This exercise might be set in the second year of a Humanities Computing, or Media Studies course. The purpose of the exercise is to demonstrate the use of Internet resources to gather research material and references to enable us to answer the question. Any conclusions evident in this case study should not be taken as being a definitive answer!

The key to this project is to establish what is meant by the term 'Digital Age', and to determine whether it applies to real life as we live it – 'work', or whether it is an invention of the media – a phrase plucked from science fiction – 'play'. A third way might be to suggest that the Digital Age is characterized by a blend of these activities. We are all familiar with the phrase, but any discussion of it must stem from a definitive interpretation.

The term 'Digital Age' must refer to a stage or period in the evolution of society, like the Industrial Revolution. We must therefore determine whether our lives are in fact changed irrevocably by the use of digital technology around us, or whether it is simply an enabling technology like plastic – you don't hear people talk about the plastic age, even though it surrounds us even in the most rural communities. This difference is crucial.

A first step might be to use a search engine to find out where the phrase is being used. HotBot returns 5,111 hits on the term, a brief scan of the first thirty reveals that the phrase is turning up as might be expected, in technology companies' Web sites, in PR companies' Web sites and in Design, Architecture and Style contexts. It also turns up 'The Emerging Digital Economy Report' instigated by the Clinton administration and the US Department of Commerce. This is likely to provide some excellent source material, containing as it does, chapters on the Digital Revolution, Building Out the Internet, Consumers in the Digital Age, Workers in the Digital Age and Challenges Ahead.

This first search has done two things; it has placed the use of the term in commercial areas which see themselves as being 'cutting edge', which suggests that the phrase may be something of a chimera, but it has also turned up a government report which is rooted in hard facts, suggesting that the Digital Age has a real life application. A reading of the report confirms what its origins suggest, that the basis of the phrase's usage is in the sense of digital economy.

We now know that the 'work' side of the argument will be expressed in terms of economic realities – commerce and employment in particular. There are other concerns expressed in the report – the role of government, law making and enforcement in particular.

The 'play' side of the argument is more complex – we are firstly interested in establishing whether the genre has reflected real life in the manner of George Orwell's *1984* or whether it is pure fantasy in the tradition of Philip K. Dick. If we can demonstrate that a part of the genre reflects real life, then we can make a compelling argument that the Digital Age is indeed upon us, because truly epochal events will be reflected in art – if we cannot, then it remains a fiction, at best a prediction.

The second stage of the search involves the use of the Humanities gateways, **Voice of the Shuttle** and **HUMBUL**. The **Voice of the Shuttle** home page contains a list of subject headings. Glancing down this list we find **Science, Technology and Culture** which looks promising, and, under a separate heading, **Cyberculture**.

The **Science, Technology and Culture** link leads us to

> **Sean Zdenek's 'Cyber: Technoculture – There's Nothing Finer, They Said'**
> http://english-www.hss.cmu.edu/cyber/

pages on the Carnegie Mellon University's English Server. Here we find most usefully, text on Baudrillard (the notion of radical play; images possessing a cultural force without reference to reality) and Vice President Al Gore's address to the International Telecommunications Union in 1994 on Global Information.

We also find a link to

> **Samuel Ebersole's 'Media Determinism in Cyberspace'**
> http://www.regent.edu/acad/schcom/rojc/mdic/md.html

pages at Regent University, which contain essays on the Early Philosophers of Technology and on Philosophical Assumptions in Cyberspace containing links to an essay and further links on the media theoritician Marshall McLuhan.

And to

The University of Iowa's Communication Studies pages on Digital Media

http://www.uiowa.edu/~commstud/resources/digitalmedia/digitaltechnology.html

which gives us a number of links to theoretical papers published in the last five years, from which we can reinforce any theoretical/philosophical arguments we might wish to use.

Browsing the **Cyberculture** section leads us to sections on the **Economics of the Net, CyberPunk Fiction** and **Business and Technology**. Under **Business and Technology**:

Information Rules: A Strategic Guide to the Network Economy
http://www.inforules.com/

a book by Carl Shapiro and Hal R. Varian can be accessed via the Commerce section of

University of California, Berkeley's Information Economy site
http://www.sims.berkeley.edu/resources/infoecon/

under **CyberPunk Fiction**:

Bruce Sterling's CyberPunk in the Nineties
gopher://gopher.well.sf.ca.us:70/00/Publications/authors/Sterling/interzone_six.txt

an essay by one of the founding fathers of the movement is found.

Paul Brian's Study Guide for William Gibson: Neuromancer (1984)
http://www.wsu.edu/~brians/science_fiction/neuromancer.html

Washington State University study guide to the seminal work of the genre, might provide some useful insights.

The link to **Journals** in the area of **Technology and Culture** will give you an idea of what is likely to be helpful – some are available on line, others will have to be ordered from the library.

HUMBUL, when searched for references to Cyberculture, Cyber and Technology fails to turn up specifically useful material. However, using the directory to browse through Film, Drama and Media Studies resources quickly takes us to

MCS

http://www.aber.ac.uk/~dgc/mcs.html

In the **IT and Telecomms** section of **MCS** we can access the following papers amongst a selection of several dozen:

'Argumentation on the Web: Challenging Traditional Notions of Communication' by Tom Formaro.

'Bakhtin and the Internet' by Terri Palmer.

'Baudrillard and the Internet' by Mark Nunes.

'As We may Think' by Vannevar Bush.

'Information Technology and Society: Issues of Control and Choice' by Lloyd Peppard.

This embarrassment of riches highlights one of the pitfalls of the Internet – information overload. At this stage, after reading a selection of these papers, we must make some decisions about what to include in the assignment.

The sources can be broadly divided into categories: Philosophy, Literature, Economics and Sociology.

- Papers falling into the Philosophy category may be useful in setting a scene for the assignment.
- Technology and Society has been a concern of philosophers for longer than the Digital Age has lasted.
- The Literature category should provide material to enable an informed discussion of the relationship between Science Fiction and Society.
- Papers falling into the Sociology category may be used to reinforce the thesis of the assignment, and much of the material found in the Sociology category may be confirmed or contradicted by material in the Economy category.

Reading through this material, a number of coherent strands should begin to emerge, and the choice is which ones are appropriate to the form of this assignment. If the assignment is short, then choose one strand as the dominant feature of the paper and make only passing reference to the existence of others. For example, from these particular papers we can isolate the following strands:

- Technology is changing the way we communicate, therefore
- Technology is changing the way we work, and
- Technology is changing the way we play.
- In the past Technology has influenced the way we work over a period of generations, now technological change affects us within weeks.
- Technology offers a virtual experience. Increasingly this virtual experience is impacting on work (teleconferencing, CMCW) and on play.
- Computer games
- Cycles in the economy are mediated by computer – stock markets, credit availability, interest rates.
- CyberPunk Fiction was originally derived from real life – like Punk Rock it emerged from a low-tech do-it-yourself culture but reflected a world where high technology was available in low-tech clothing. It was the availability of the Xerox copying machine that allowed the 'zine ethos to flourish.

It is tempting to think that the work is now done – unfortunately this is not the case. While some of the material accessed here will be serious academic work, you still need to track down common citations and this can only be done through your library. The point of doing this is that an assignment of this nature is not just about recycling other people's ideas, but it should also be about checking the provenance of their ideas and the interpretation of these ideas in the context of your own work. By re-reading commonly cited work, you may find new or different interpretations of the work, which will add to the value of your own assignment.

8.5 Referencing Web texts

Many texts found on the Web will also be available in printed form. If the text is extracted from a journal or conference proceedings, then it should be referenced in the conventional way. If it is extracted from a Web site and there are no obvious pointers to another source, then it should be referenced as such. There is no agreed format across all universities for this, but it is essential at least to reference the URL and the descriptive name of the material. For example:

References

Wright C	Pulling Focus on the WWW
	http://www.unl.ac.uk/~cwright/publish.html, 1997
Wright C. and Jones R.	A Novel Architecture for WWW-based Learning,
	5th Annual Conference on the Teaching of Computing, Dublin, August 1997

In the example, the first reference is to a seminar paper, published on the WWW. The second reference is to a paper published on the WWW, but also published in print format in the proceedings of the named conference.

To summarize, if the paper has ever been published in paper form then the reference should be to the first printed version. Only if the paper has never been published except on the Web, should the reference be to a Web site. The reason is that references form a paper trail for researchers. If you find a paper that contains some interesting ideas, then look for the references. The printed versions can always be ordered through a university library (through the British Library ultimately). Until every discipline is equally represented on the Web, the library will remain the primary source of information. A reference to a Web site can only be tracked down by those with access to the Web.

8.6 Summary

In this chapter we have looked closely at two completely different types of project, and seen how we can use the Internet to gather research materials quickly, and with practice, easily.

Some rules have emerged:
- Devote a set period of time to information gathering.
- Gather information first then sort it.
- Gather information in stages – from the general to the specific.

- Make sure your sources are reliable.
- You drive the process, be ruthless about discarding irrelevant information.
- Back up your Web-based research by looking up commonly cited sources in your library. Read these papers.

8.7 Exercises

These exercises are not intended to be subject specific. Using the methods outlined here, try to assemble enough resources to answer these questions. Every one of them is possible to answer directly using resources from this book.

1 Gather resources, including photographs, texts of speeches and recordings for a multimedia presentation on the American War of Independence.

2 Ridley Scott, the director of *Bladerunner* has a brother, Tony; Name two films directed by Tony Scott.

3 Bedlam, the famous London asylum for the insane is graphically represented in the series of paintings by Hogarth, called the Rake's Progress. How different was the reality to the way it was portrayed by Hogarth, and what evidence is there to support the view that it was different?

4 *Pulp Fiction* has redefined the gangland thriller with its use of extreme violence, snappy dialogue and oblique references to other films. In the 1960s, British director Nicholas Roeg made a film starring Mick Jagger and James Fox that so shocked Warner Brothers that they delayed its release until 1970. What was the name of this film, who was the script writer and what other films did he make?

Part Four

GETTING TO GRIPS WITH THE TECHNOLOGY

This section of the book is primarily aimed at first time users. It introduces a standard set of Internet applications, outlines how they work and explains how to get the best from them. The applications are arranged in a logical order:

- Ping may be used to ascertain whether a remote computer is accessible.

- Telnet may be used to access a remote computer.

- FTP may be used to transfer files to or from a remote computer.

- E-mail is used to send messages from one computer to one or many others,

- Usenet news is a many-to-many e-mail based connection.

- IRC is a synchronous many-to-many communication.

Each application discussed is self-contained. You do not need to know how Ping works in order to use e-mail – but you might want to use Ping some time to see why your e-mails are not getting through!

9 | INTERNET SERVICES

9.1 Aims of this chapter

This chapter introduces some basic Internet services and explains how they work. In terms of your day to day experience of using the Internet, some of these may be used infrequently. However, they help to build a clear picture of what happens when you use various Internet applications, and understanding the technology will help you to get the best from it.

Examples are based on a standard set up using Windows 95/98 or Windows NT.

9.2 Ping

Ping is used to check whether an Internet address is accessible and gives information about the connection. Ping sends a series of messages across a network and times the interval occurring before an acknowledgement is received. You only need to know an address of a remote computer to use Ping.

The illustration (Figure 9.1) shows Ping, having recorded an average time of approximately 130 milliseconds for four sets of data to be returned from a remote server.

To invoke Ping:

    Click the **Start** button

    Choose **Run**

    Type **Ping** (hostname)   e.g.. Ping www.myComputer.co.uk

where hostname is the address of the computer you are checking. If the request times out, you can assume that the computer is not accessible. If

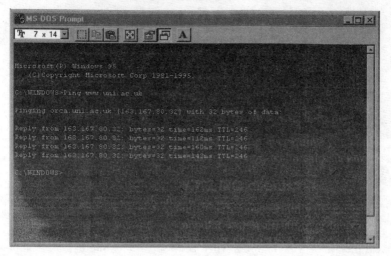

Figure 9.1 Ping

you get a reply similar to the one in the illustration, the computer has responded to your request.

9.3 Telnet

Telnet is a program that allows the user to log in to a remote system and use a command line interface to work on that computer via the local keyboard. Often this is used by Unix users to access their own accounts from any computer. There is another popular use for Telnet in education – connection to library catalogues. As well as your own college library, you can use Telnet to contact literally thousands of libraries all over the world.

The WWW is rapidly providing visual interfaces to programs that have traditionally been the domain of Telnet clients such as OPAC (On-Line Public Access Catalog), the library system which is used by virtually all university and civic libraries for remote connection.

OPAC is a database package, usually accessed via Telnet. It is possible to search library catalogues, reserve books (if you are a member), extend loans etc. all through a simple VT100 type interface running a simple menu system over a series of screens.

The best Telnet library resource is called Hytelnet, developed and maintained by Peter Scott of Berkeley University. Hytelnet is scheduled for close down at the time of writing, but will be replaced by a larger resource. It is currently accessible on the WWW and in addition to information and advice about Telnet itself, contains the Telnet address and login details of thousands of universities, grouped by location or by name.

A Telnet session works in a similar way to FTP (see below).

> Click on the **Start** button
>
> Choose **Run**
>
> Type **Telnet** (address)   e.g.. Telnet locis.loc.gov (Library of Congress)
>
> Login

The screen will now prompt you about what to do next – the screen in Figure 9.2 is from the American Library of Congress.

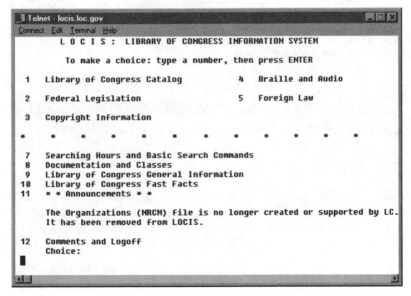

Figure 9.2 Telnet: the Library of Congress

A slightly archaic but useful program accessible by Telnet is ARCHIE. This is an interactive search program that returns a list of all the FTP sites that contain a file of a specified name.

For example, if we wanted to download a copy of PKZIP, the shareware
file compression program, and we did not have access to a Web browser,
ARCHIE will tell us where to find it and what directory to look in once we
have connected via FTP. Figure 9.3 shows the result of a search by ARCHIE
at Imperial College, London.

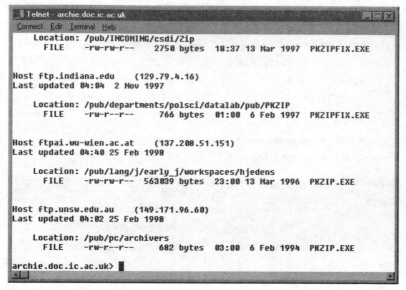

Figure 9.3 ARCHIE

9.4 FTP

FTP or File Transfer Protocol is a method of transferring files from one
computer to another across a network. Servers exist which act as
warehouses full of public domain software. These are known as FTP servers
and you can log onto them using anonymous FTP.

Suppose we wanted to download a copy of Netscape Navigator from
Netscape Corporation. We can do this by opening the Windows FTP client.

> Click on the **Start** button
>
> Choose **Run**...
>
> Type **ftp ftp.netscape.com**

Note that ftp is typed twice here. This is because most FTP servers are called 'ftp' for convenience, the second 'ftp' is part of the address. The command used to invoke the ftp program is also ftp, it takes as an argument the address of the server you are trying to contact.

The server will prompt you for a user name. Type

    anonymous

your password is your e-mail address.

If you have done this successfully, you should be looking at the screen shown in Figure 9.4.

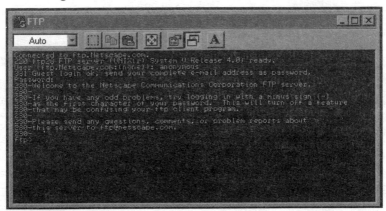

Figure 9.4 FTP

From here, it is a question of using the FTP command set to navigate through the directory structure to the required file and retrieve it.

Command	Effect
dir	Print directory
cd *public*	Change Directory on the remote machine (to *public*)
lcd *C:\Temp*	Change directory on the local machine to *C:\Temp*
cd ..	Move one step up the remote directory tree
ascii	Set data type to ascii
binary	Set data type to binary
hash	Put hash marks on the screen while data is transferred
get *filename*	Retrieve file *filename*
bye	Goodbye (closes connection)

Other useful commands include

Command	Effect
put *filename*	Send file *filename*
mget **.gif*	Get all the files with the extension *.gif*
mput **.gif*	Put all the files with the extension *.gif*
mkdir incoming	Create directory called incoming on the remote machine
delete	Delete file on remote machine
mdelete **.gif*	Delete all *gifs* on the remote machine
rename *file1 file2*	Rename *file1 file2*
?	Help
bell	Causes a bell to sound when a file transfer is complete

Typically anonymous FTP servers would not permit the use of commands that manipulate files on the server. However, if you are making a Web site and uploading a selection of files, the chances are that you will find these useful.

It pays to exercise extreme caution when uploading files; it is too easy to upload the wrong version or to upload in the wrong format. For this reason, it is worth backing up all files with the **rename** command

rename intro.htm intro.old

Now, if you have uploaded a corrupted version of **intro.htm**, you only have to delete it and change the name back again to restore your file.

If you upload a picture with the type ASCII, it will not be served over the Web. so always check that you have specified the correct file type before sending it. Similarly, you won't be able to run a binary executable if you have just downloaded it as an ASCII file.

Apart from downloading free software and maintaining your Web site, another constructive use of FTP is to retrieve library lists for use with Telnet. Most universities operate an inter-library loan system, so if you are searching for a rare title, library lists give you a chance to track it down, wherever it is. For example,

ftp ftp.funet.fi
Path: /pub/doc/library/*

to see the directory listing of library resources at funet.

You can retrieve the files and read them at leisure, in preparation for later Telnet sessions.

9.4.1 File types: compression and decompression

One of the major considerations when downloading files is speed and size. This has led to the widespread use of archiving and compression routines. Archiving refers to the practice of bundling a collection of files into a single file.

Compression refers to the practice of reducing the size of a file so that it will download faster. This is done in a number of cunning ways that are way beyond the scope of this book – if you're really interested, there is lots of information about compression algorithms available on the Internet!

Most Windows compression utilities such as WinZip allow compression and archiving to be done simultaneously – if only it were always so simple. The Internet was built on Unix machines and because of this, you can expect many of the files available for download to be in a Unix-only format. They will often be archived with one program and compressed with another thus ensuring that the command to render these files usable is unintelligible to all but the most determined Unix enthusiast. This section will attempt to demystify the arcana of Unix compression routines as well as introducing the use of shareware Windows programs and giving pointers on where to obtain them. Unless you are studying computer science, however, it is unlikely that you will have much need for Unix.

Firstly, we will look at the file suffix and see how you can tell from the filename, how it has been compressed, and what you will need to decompress it.

File extension	Created by	Recovered by...
.zip	WinZip, PKZip	WinZip, PKZip
.Z	compress	uncompress
.gz	gzip (UNIX only)	gunzip
.tar	tar (UNIX archive)	tar, zcat
.uu	uuencode	uudecode
.hqx	BinHex (Mac)	BinHex, Stuffit
.sit	Stuffit (Mac)	Stuffit

These addresses probably represent the best sources of shareware utilities:

Tucows

http://tucows.ameritel.net/   Windows only

Jumbo!

http://www.luckman.com/yp/0138/013877.html   PC, Mac, OS2

Download.com

http://www.download.com   PC only

Tucows is notable for having mirror sites (local archives) all over the world, so to decrease download time, you can navigate to your nearest archive direct from their opening page.

Figure 9.5 shows WinZip, inspecting a zipped archive called opconwin.zip. The archive only contains one file, an .html file called Open Controller Window.htm. The file is 9.191 kb in its normal state, but after zipping, is only 3.225 kb or 65% smaller. This means that if you are connecting from home, via a modem, your phone bill for downloading this file is 65% cheaper if the file is compressed!

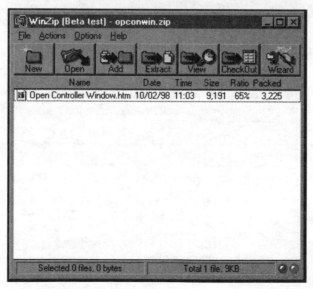

Figure 9.5 WinZip

The program is blissfully simple to use – to restore an archive to normal size, simply click on the **Extract** button and follow the instructions. You will be asked to specify a directory to extract the archive to, then wait until the program has done its job. To open a single file in an archive, click on the **Open** button. To create an archive, put all your files into a single directory, click on the **New** button and follow the instructions. You will be asked to specify a name for the archive and to indicate by highlighting which files you want to include.

The .zip format is by far the most widely used, and WinZip for Windows or PKZip for DOS are widely available. They are both shareware, which means that you should contact the authors and pay for them if you intend to keep using them. If you use a PC, you will certainly need to get hold of a copy of WinZip.

The shareware principle is still used by some companies, but more usually demonstration versions of programs are available that are disabled in some way until a key is entered which is only available on payment being received by the vendor. CompuServe set up a mechanism by which the shareware would be registered through the appropriate forum, and the cost would be added on to the CompuServe bill for that month, which neatly side-stepped the fears concerning Internet security.

Unix (and Linux) users generally use a two step process to compress files. First a program called **tar** (designed for use with tape back ups: **t**ape **ar**chive) is used to build an archive holding all the files under one directory name. Let's take an imaginary directory called **myThesis** into which I have copied all the files I want to include in an archive. First, navigate to the directory immediately above myThesis.

tar cf myThesisArchive.tar myThesis/*

tar invokes the tar program, the switches **c** and **f** tell it that we are creating an archive in a file,

myThesis/* tells it to include all the files in the subdirectory called myThesis.

The resulting file is called **myThesisArchive.tar**. This file will still be far too large, so we will use **gzip** to compress the file.

gzip myThesisArchive.tar

gives us a compressed file called **myThesisArchive.tar.gz**.

To disentangle Unix files compressed with **gzip** and archived with **tar**, do the following.

    tar xvzf myThesisArchive.tar.gz

This will unzip and extract the files to a directory called **myThesis** which will be created in the current directory, containing the original files in their original form.

The first part of the command is as follows: **tar** runs the tar program, the switches **xvzf** indicate that we want to extract the archive, in verbose mode, unzipping the files and forcing a restore on all files. Verbose mode causes the computer to list the files onscreen as they are being unpacked.

Alternatively, this can be done in two steps, first unzip the files:

    gunzip myThesisArchive.tar.gz

this leaves you with a file called **myThesisArchive.tar**, about 60% bigger than the previous version; then unpack the archive:

    tar -xvf myThesisArchive.tar

You now have the contents of the archive restored to their original form i.e. uncompressed, in a directory called **myThesis**.

9.5 E-mail

E-mail is short for 'electronic mail'. E-mail is used to send messages between individual users and to post messages to multi-user forums such as Usenet news or Listserv mailing groups. A message sent by e-mail will not arrive instantly, but usually arrives within a few seconds of being sent if the destination is physically local. If the destination is geographically distant, the message will have to traverse several networks, and like any journey, (network) traffic conditions will affect the time of arrival. It is still likely to be measured in seconds rather than hours.

The e-mail system is based around the use of clients and servers. The client is the software used on the PC to read and write mail, the server distributes the mail to the clients, or forwards it from the clients on a network to a Mail Transfer Agent for forwarding to a remote recipient. Each network has a mail server, to which all mail addressed to users on that network is delivered.

Arrangements for reading mail vary from system to system. Nowadays POP3 and IMAP mail clients enable the user to download messages from a central mail server. It is likely that a university will provide a mail client compatible with one or both of these protocols. Alternatively, users may be required to log on to a separate mail server and read mail remotely, as is the case with VAX mail, a system which is still very common in universities in the UK.

Users interface to mail in the same way, whatever the system. Mail is viewed first by a list of subject lines, individual messages can be chosen and read at the users' convenience. In a Unix or VMS system, typing

mail

at the command prompt will invoke a mail client which will display a list of numbered mail subject lines. The subject line is a descriptive phrase inserted by the sender. Typing the number next to the subject line will cause the client to display the message.

Unix networks in colleges will almost certainly feature a mail program called Pine which was developed at the University of Washington in 1989. It is unusual amongst computer programs in that it is both good, robust and free. It was designed specifically for administrative staff who were not accomplished users, and the results reflect this priority – menu driven, it boasts a user friendly interface with copious help facilities and allows the user to create folders, navigate between them, compose new messages and create address books with considerable ease. It would be no exaggeration to say that Pine is without peer amongst Unix utilities. To invoke the Pine menu, simply type **pine** at the command prompt, noting the lowercase 'p'.

Macintosh users will probably find themselves using Eudora, a full featured GUI driven mail client, while PC/Windows users will be spoilt for choice. Chapter 10 provides a detailed description of Windows based e-mail use. All e-mail clients provide the same base set of facilities as Pine.

9.6 Usenet news

Usenet news builds on e-mail. Where e-mail is used to send messages between individuals, Usenet news exploits a method of sending mail to multiple addresses. In simple terms, Usenet news is like a computerized bar without the alcohol – people have animated discussions with total strangers, united only by a common interest in the topic under discussion.

In fact Usenet is composed of thousands of groups, divided hierarchically by topic. Users subscribe to a group and read the articles. Both Netscape and Microsoft have built news readers into their e-mail facility. This is slightly confusing as they are historically entirely separate entities, but it does make a certain amount of sense to access a newsgroup through the e-mail client. Chapter 11 gives a detailed look at the use of news readers, as well as lists of newsgroups.

9.7 IRC

IRC, or Internet Relay Chat, is as close as it gets on the Internet to real time communication between large numbers of people. E-mail and Usenet news are examples of asynchronous communication, where users can read and reply to messages at their leisure. Whereas IRC could be described as synchronous communication because exchanges occur almost instantaneously as they would by telephone.

Another example of a client–server system, IRC is based on a number of chat clients communicating with a single chat server, which copies all the messages out in the order in which they are received to all clients. Messages are listed on the client screen, preceded by the name or alias of the person sending the message, so the output resembles a play with no discernible plot.

If this sounds confusing, it isn't – just as at a party, you manage to concentrate on a single thread of conversation amongst many, you will find yourself looking out for messages from the person or people that you are conversing with.

The chat server acts as a host for a number of channels, most of which are available to the ordinary user. A channel can be selected from the Channels Folder and when joined, operates in its own window. A single client can simultaneously be connected to many channels.

Figure 9.6 shows one of the most popular IRC clients, mIRC – the interface is divided into separate windows, one monitoring the connection to the IRC server, and another monitoring a particular channel – in this case the Windows 95 channel. Input from the user is entered into the text field at

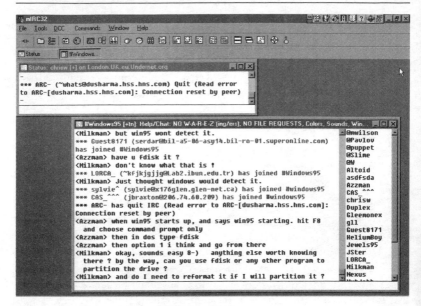

Figure 9.6 Internet Relay Chat (mIRC)

the bottom of the channel window and submitted by pressing the carriage return on the keyboard. It will then be printed in the channel window next to your nickname. The list of users on the channel can be seen at the right-hand side of the channel window. It is customary for people to assume some kind of alias, or nickname. This serves the dual purpose of hiding your gender from the participants (like any party, IRC plays host to a proportion of pests and women can be subjected to irritatingly persistent harassment) and stimulating conversation.

There are hundreds of channels to choose from, some devoted entirely to beginners, others to specific interests such as (inevitably) computers and football. Soccer enthusiasts often set up a channel on match days, monitoring the match as it is played. This (if you enjoy soccer) is excellent fun, combining the bar room humour of the terraces with the excitement of listening to the match on the radio, without the inconvenience of paying to get in, getting soaked to the skin and queuing for hours in the car park!

If any of this sounds like a constructive way to spend time, the following is a guide to getting started on IRC.

9.7.1 IRC Documentation

There is a truly incredible amount of information available on IRC, reflecting its status as one of the most popular activities next to browsing. Many of the clients available for download come equipped with an IRC Intro and FAQ (list of Frequently Asked Questions – and their answers). However, the IRC Help Home page at

http://www.irchelp.org/

is a gateway to everything you could ever wish to know about IRC, from primers for non-technical users to Unix scripts and RFCs for experts.

9.7.2 IRC clients

mIRC is almost certainly the easiest IRC client to set up and use – extremely popular with users all over the world, the Web site at **www.mirc.co.uk** is mirrored in the USA, The Netherlands, Italy, Kuwait, Argentina, Brazil, South Africa and Australia, which gives some idea of the program's popularity. The difference between mIRC and most other IRC clients is that mIRC deals with setting up through a series of dialogue boxes, and quizzes your computer for much of the detail required. It also comes with a menu of available servers, so setting up and making the first connection can be accomplished in a couple of minutes.

Other IRC clients well worth looking at are

- **IRC Gold** available from
  http://www.erols.com/smerchant/
- **Pirch98** available from
  http://www.bcpl.lib.md.us/~frappa/pirch.html
- and finally **VIRC98** available from
  http://www.megalith.co.uk/virc/

VIRC98 is notable for being integrated into the Windows desktop like a Microsoft Office application. Apart from its voice and video conferencing features and clickable hyperlinks which automatically invoke your browser, it is fully extensible, supporting scripting languages JavaScript and Python, as well as its own object oriented language, ObjectViRCScript. One for the technically ambitious definitely, but also usable by beginners.

9.7.3 IRC servers

An IRC server is usually part of a network of servers. There are dozens of IRC networks, but the ones which are most rewarding for the beginner are those with the largest number of servers, as they will reach the largest number of people.

There are four networks, collectively known as the big four, which account for most of the IRC traffic. These are:

EFnet

EFNet servers can be found in Australia, Canada, Finland, France, Israel, The Netherlands, Norway, Sweden, UK and the USA. This is the largest IRC network and the one many people think of as 'IRC'. A full list of servers, can be found at

http://www.irchelp.org/irchelp/networks/servers/efnet.html

Undernet

Undernet servers can be found in Belgium, Canada, France, Germany, The Netherlands, New Zealand, Norway, Spain, UK and the USA. A full list of servers, can be found at

http://servers.undernet.org/

IRCnet

IRCNet servers can be found in Australia, Austria, Belgium, Czech Republic, Denmark, Estonia, Finland, France, Germany, Greece, Hungary, Iceland, Israel, Italy, Japan, Latvia, Lithuania, Malaysia, The Netherlands, Norway, Poland, Russia, Slovakia, Slovenia, Spain, Sweden, Switzerland, UK and the USA.

The majority of these servers are former EFnet servers, having separated from the EFnet in July 1996. This network claims to be the 'original' IRC. Many of the most popular channels here are 'national' channels, providing a 'home from home' for many ex-pats. A full list of available servers can be found at

http://www.irchelp.org/irchelp/networks/servers/ircnet.html

DALnet

DALNet servers can be found in Australia, Canada, Norway, Sweden, UK, and the USA. It was originally created by users of the EFnet's #startrek channel, but has diversified into a far more varied and interesting selection. A full list of available servers can be found at

http://www.dal.net/

9.7.4 IRC channels

The real business of IRC, conversation with other users, takes place on a channel. Each server supports a number of channels with descriptive names, prefaced by a hash sign, such as

#newbie – for new users

#Win95 – for Windows 95 questions and advice

#Leeds – for Leeds United soccer supporters on match days

#irchelp – for help on IRC

#cybercafe – for socializing

Every channel has an 'op' who is responsible for maintaining the channel. The op has the power to exclude people from channels, so try to exercise a level of decorum appropriate to the channel you are in. In other words, acting like you are in **#hottub** when you are in **#Win95** will probably get you unceremoniously slung off the channel!

Most IRC clients open up with a connection window, allowing input in a text field at the base. IRC has a set of commands, which must be prefaced by a forward slash (/). If upon connecting to a network, I input the command

/list

I could expect to see a list of the publicly available channels. If I want to join **#Leeds** I would input

/join #Leeds

Most modern Windows based clients make joining a channel a simple matter of selecting one from a list; however, sometimes the command line approach is quicker. A list of the most useful commands is given in section 9.7.6.

9.7.5 IRC client configuration

By this time, you have either moved on to another chapter or are aching to join the IRC world. First you will need to configure the client you have chosen from section 9.7.2. You will need to supply some information about your computer and the address of the server you are connecting to. Typically this will be entered in a series of dialogue boxes, invoked from the set-up menu.

Computer information: IP address

Server information: address + Port number (usually 6667)

Personal information: Name, e-mail address, nickname, 2nd nickname

The IP address of your computer can be obtained from the TCP/IP configuration dialogue in the Control Panel under Windows. Choose a Server from the lists referenced in section 9.7.3, one that is geographically local to you, and choose two nicknames. The reason for this is that most of the obvious ones are quite popular and there is only one instance of a nickname allowed in a channel at a time.

9.7.6 IRC command reference

This is a list of useful commands you might run while chatting.

Command	Effect
/join #channelname	join a channel
/help commandname	shows help on the command commandname
/whois nickname	gets the E-Mail address of a specified nickname
/me description	'stage' instruction to group e.g.. /me snores loudly
/ignore nickname	filters all messages from specified nickname
/nick nickname	changes your nickname to specified nickname
/msg nickname	sends private message to specified nickname
/query nickname	starts private conversation in separate window
/part	leave current channel
/bye	disconnects from server

9.8 Summary

After reading this chapter you should be able to use a basic set of applications including Ping, Telnet, FTP and IRC. You should know how to use Telnet to access an ARCHIE server and what to do when you have accessed it. You should also be able to describe the functions of e-mail and Usenet news.

9.9 Exercises

1. Use Ping to see how long it takes to send a message to your university Web server (probably **www.universityname.edu** or **www.universityname.ac.uk**).

2. Use Telnet to access your university/college library and discover whether *Night Train* by Martin Amis is available.

3. Use Telnet to contact an ARCHIE server and locate a file called *WinZip.exe*.

4. Use FTP to download a copy of *WinZip.exe*.

5. Run *WinZip.exe* and when it is installed on your computer, use it to compress your subject assignments into an archive.

6. Download an IRC client, configure it and find an interesting channel.

10 USING E-MAIL

10.1 Aims of this chapter

The aim of this chapter is to explain the use of e-mail and to enable the first time user to avoid many of the pitfalls that immediately identify the new user or 'newbie'.

10.2 Why use e-mail?

E-mail is one of the fastest growing forms of communication available. There are good reasons for this. E-mail provides something that neither the post or the telephone can hope to emulate – the ability to transfer, almost instantaneously, digital files to other computer users.

There are other significant advantages – e-mail is an asynchronous form of communication – as is the mail service. E-mail, because it is so fast, allows the recipient to make a choice between reading it immediately or leaving it until later. Unlike the telephone, it is not intrusive – there is no risk of interrupting someone by sending them an e-mail.

10.3 How to get the most out of e-mail

The best resource on the Internet for learning about e-mail is undoubtedly Mary Houten-Kemp's Everything E-Mail at

http://everythingemail.net/

This resource (Figure 10.1) contains links to almost everything you need to know about using e-mail, including good style guides and technical descriptions.

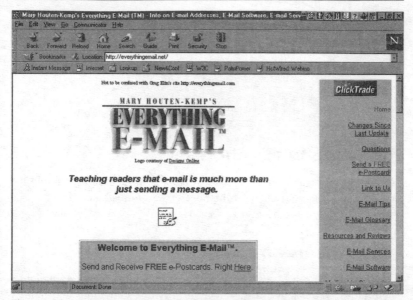

Figure 10.1 The Everything E-Mail Resource

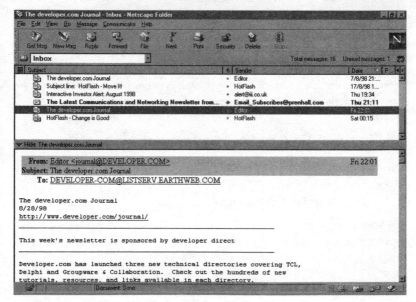

Figure 10.2 Netscape Messenger, e-mail client

10.3.1 Student accounts

Typically a student will automatically receive an e-mail address when they are given an account on the college network. This address will take the form:

username@someCollege.ac.uk

where the account is held at a university or college in England, and will be used by anyone who wants to send you an e-mail. In Figure 10.3, a person sending an e-mail to you would put this address in the 'To:' text box. Similarly, if they have received an e-mail from you, it would appear in the 'Sender' column. This is why it is important to sign e-mails with your real name – it's hard to identify certain network addresses. Figure 10.2 shows Netscape Messenger which is typical of many Windows based e-mail clients using POP3 to retrieve mail on demand from a central location.

The client is divided into two areas, one in which the whole list of messages is displayed, another in which the highlighted message can be viewed. The list area is arranged in columns, giving the Subject line of the message (usually a brief description), the author, the time received and the priority if any. This arrangement allows the user to read the most interesting messages first. It is usually possible to save messages into different folders, constructed in the same way as Internet bookmarks, for reading later.

Figure 10.3 shows the interface used for sending a message, accessed in this client by pressing the **New Msg** button, visible on the toolbar in Figure 10.2.

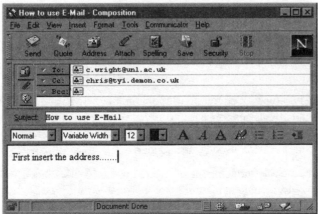

Figure 10.3 Composing an e-mail in Netscape Messenger

The address field offers three different categories: **To:** which indicates the primary destination, **Cc:** which indicates the addresses of those people to whom the message is copied, and **Bcc:** which allows the sender to 'blind copy' the message to somebody else, without the primary recipient's knowledge.

The Subject line contains a descriptive phrase designed to help the recipient decide whether to read the message or save it until later. You will soon find that you are receiving enough e-mail to prove the value of a decent Subject line!

10.3.2 Address books

Most e-mail clients will feature an address book utility, allowing you to store addresses and include them in the addressee field by pointing and clicking. This useful utility is sadly not portable between clients, and is unlikely to be available on college networks at present.

10.3.3 Binary attachments

It is possible to attach files to an e-mail message. This means that you can 'enclose' the draft of a project report in an e-mail to your tutor for example. Most university systems will have an upper limit on the size of attachments, as sending a multi-megabyte message through the e-mail system will have the same effect as driving a team of camels through a modern city centre – it will bring the speed of other traffic down to a crawl.

Because e-mail is supported by its own set of protocols, anything which is attached to an e-mail must be encoded into ASCII format for transmission and un-encoded at the other end. Because of the proliferation of e-mail clients and the operating systems on which they run, this can lead to incompatibilities between sender and receiver.

There are two types of encoding in common use, MIME and UUENCODE. Not all mail clients support both, so if you receive a message that contains what looks like raw computer code, you should try to ascertain what type of encoding has been used by the sender.

A MIME encoded attachment of a picture, sent with Pine from a Unix system would include something like this at the top of the file:

Content-Type: IMAGE/JPEG; name="Network.jpg"

Content-Transfer-Encoding: BASE64

Content-ID: <Pine.SOL.5.83.568207445813.56930B@comp.myuni.edu>

Content-Description:

A uuencoded file would contain a phrase

begin 666 Network.jpg

before turning into human illegible code.

A utility called **mpack** can be used to code and decode MIME based files and **uudecode** can be used to decode uuencoded files. For information on how to find and retrieve these utilities, refer to Chapter 9, section 9.4 on FTP. Alternatively, you can mail the sender and ask them to re-send the message to an account where an appropriate mail client is available.

10.3.4 E-mail clients

Both Internet Explorer and Netscape come with their own e-mail clients, but many people prefer to use a separate application. There are hundreds, literally, of e-mail clients available, but the most popular ones across all platforms are

- For Unix, Pine (freeware)
- For Windows, Pegasus (freeware), Eudora
- For Macintosh, Eudora

All of these mail clients provide a basic set of utilities allowing the use of attachments, mail folders and filtering (automatic storage of incoming mail into appropriate folders).

10.4 E-mail etiquette

There is a well established etiquette with e-mail, aimed at making the impersonal medium more friendly and accessible. Here are some of the most important elements. Always sign your e-mail with your name. Your User name will appear in the 'from' column in the message list, but it is unlikely that anyone will want to take the trouble to decipher it!

You need not begin your message with the formal 'Dear ...', a simple 'Hi' will do for friends, or just the first name for colleagues.

Always start a new line after 60 – 70 characters. The reason for this is that there are a number of different mail clients available, and while some will automatically wrap text as it is entered, they don't always insert the new line character. The result is that your 500 word message appears to the reader in a single line – the chances are high that they won't read it. You don't need to count the characters, just keep each line short, as if you are writing a note on paper.

There are also a number of things to avoid in e-mail. Typing messages IN CAPITAL LETTERS is known as shouting and is usually done unintentionally by beginners. It is considered to be extremely boorish – like somebody shouting in a quiet conversation.

Irony does not come across well in short messages displayed (usually) in plain courier type. Remember that your well honed turns of phrase may delight your friends, but your friends know you from experience, and even they may not get the joke when all they can see is the printed word. Try to avoid irony and sarcasm.

Do not send anonymous and offensive mail to anyone – e-mail messages can be traced back to their sender and you could be removed from the network if you make a habit of this. More significantly, there is a story concerning someone who thought it would be amusing to send a death threat to the President of the USA. The FBI were not so amused and the sender is currently in jail. This type of prank is never amusing – after all you can hardly share the joke.

Do not lord it over new users. The Internet is evolving faster than any one person can keep track of, therefore we are all newcomers to an extent. If you think you know it all, you are wrong and likely to remain ignorant – people like nothing better than tripping up a know all.

Do not send credit card details by e-mail. While much of the panic about Internet security is ill founded, there is no point in taking unnecessary risks with your credit card.

Do not reply to lengthy messages including the whole message and adding a single line of comment. This is a waste of bandwidth (connection time/computer space) and the recipient's time. When replying to an e-mail, edit the original so that you can be seen to be replying to specific points.

10.4.1 Smileys

Smileys are sometimes used to indicate feelings in electronic mail. They are formed by the juxtaposition of punctuation marks, which, when viewed sideways slightly resemble a face. For example

Happy	:-)
Sad	:-(
Shocked	:-o
Wink	;-)
Drunk	;-}

If you must use irony, then you might also want to use a 'smiley' to indicate the joke. For example

```
Professor Wittgenstein was sporting a particularly
splendid cardigan today ;-)
```

would indicate to the recipient, that you probably think cardigans are beyond the pale. Leave out the smiley and there is a very real danger that you might end up as the unwilling recipient of a matching cardigan at your next birthday!

10.4.2 Acronyms

The world is full of acronyms and the computing world is responsible for most of them – if you use e-mail a lot, you will come across a number of apparently unfathomable acronyms which are in common usage. The interesting thing about acronym use in the context of e-mail is that the practice has evolved alongside the smiley as a way of signifying irony – it replaces body language. The practice is still evolving, so this list is far from definitive, but some of these will certainly be a help.

- **IMHO** In my humble opinion – often used to calm things down – 'IMHO we are all guilty of acronym overload!'

- **FWIW** For what it's worth – rather more contentious than IMHO – 'FWIW noone in this group knows how to use acronyms appropriately.'

- **FCS** For Christ's sake – a lot more contentious than IMHO – 'FCS has this group gone acronym crazy?'

- **WTF**   What the F*** – extreme impatience or resignation
              – 'WTF are you blathering about?' or 'You lot know
              best … still, WTF.'
- **ROFL**   Rolls on floor laughing – used as a 'stage direction'
              to signify mirth.
- **AFAIK**   As far as I know - Lacks the ironic status of IMHO,
              used to signify that the user is not the world's
              leading expert.

10.5   Mailing lists (Listserv etc.)

Mailing lists are small highly specialized discussion groups. Once
subscribed to a list, any message sent to the list address is sent out by the
list server to everyone on the list, as an e-mail. The number of people
subscribing to a typical mailing list is between one and several hundred.
Usenet news on the other hand is likely to be read by several thousand
people.

Mailing lists tend to operate like small communities; you have a relationship
with the people on the list, so there are some ground rules that apply equally
to Listserv and Usenet news. Most importantly, don't join a group and
immediately flood it with messages. People will treat you exactly the same
as if you gatecrashed a party and tried to dominate the conversation – the
only difference is that you will get to read their opinions about you, as
they will be circulated to everyone on the list. The best tactic is to join and
get a sense of the list over a few days, before you make a contribution –
this practice is known as 'lurking'.

Mailing lists will have an administrator or moderator who is in charge of
the list, and makes sure that it runs smoothly. Joining a list is a fully
automated process, involving sending a message to a computer program,
for example Listserv or Majordomo.

Listserv is actually a List Administration product made by a company
called L-Soft International, their Web site contains a list of 18,219 publicly
accessible mailing lists, so there is plenty of choice. Education provides a
huge user base for Listserv, so much so that the term has become
synonymous with the medium. Other list administration tools include
Majordomo, which is free and increasingly widely used, and Listproc. All

these products are exclusively e-mail based. There are browser based list administration tools, but at the time of writing, these have not showed the reliability or the user base of the three mentioned here.

The L-Soft International Web site at **http://www.lsoft.com/lists/ listref.html** is the home of Listserv and contains a search engine that allows the user to search for lists on specific topics. An example search for music related lists turned up 82 lists covering classical music to seventies punk rock and all points in between (see Figure 10.4).

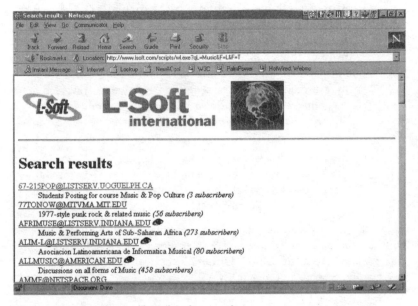

Figure 10.4 Public mailing lists for music

Other sites that contain useful mailing list resources, including detailed instructions on how to join and where to look for lists include

- **http://www.webcom.com/impulse/list.html**   Comprehensive listings, including detailed HowTos for the three most popular list servers Listserv, Majordomo and Listproc.
- **http://www.screen.com/start/guide/email.html** Life on the Internet site, aimed at beginners and providing HowTos, software reviews and downloads, as well as links to the most popular list directories.

- **http://www.nlc-bnc.ca/ifla/I/training/listserv/lists.htm**
  Very businesslike site, explaining how e-mail lists work, how
  to administer them and providing links to other sites of
  interest.

List directories include

- **http://n2h2.com/KOVACS/** The Directory of Scholarly and
  Professional E-Conferences, contains lists of academic and
  professional subject related lists – a gold-mine for researchers.

- **http://www.liszt.com/** Liszt – the Mailing List Directory is
  arranged in classic directory style, a list of categories allowing
  the user to drill down into more specialised areas. A search
  through the music listings revealed an extraordinary
  proliferation of lists focusing on seventies progressive rock.
  More usefully perhaps, a search on Humanities revealed a
  staggering 239 lists, while searching on Literature revealed
  29 specialist lists ranging from Anne Rice (inevitably) to
  Medieval Texts – Philology, Codicology and Technology.

- **http://tile.net/listserv/** Tile.net is comparable to Liszt, but
  broader categories result in more time spent trawling through
  lists of lists. Literature here is bundled with writing, and
  returns over 100 possible lists.

These directories will lead to a page including specific instructions on
how to join the group you have selected. For example this information
was gleaned from the L-Soft Directory, concerning the Library and
Information Science in Canada list.

```
List name:
        BIBCANLIB-L
Host name:
        INFOSERV.NLC-BNC.CA
Subscribers:
        639
```

To subscribe, send mail to Listserv@INFOSERV.NLC-
BNC.CA with the command (paste it!):

```
        SUBSCRIBE BIBCANLIB-L
```

This is typical of most mailing list joining procedures – usually you will subscribe by sending a message containing the line

subscribe ListName

where ListName is the name of the mail group (many servers are host to multiple mail groups). In return you will receive a message confirming your membership and a set of instructions on how to leave the group, suspend your membership whilst on holiday, receive only the digest (all messages in one file). This exchange of messages is entirely computer administered, so make sure that you copy the subscription command exactly!

Remember, make sure you file the instructions for future reference – there are few things more irritating than people sending their unsubscribe messages to the list itself, rather than the administration address they will have received on joining the list. There is no surer way to invite a flaming! Mailing lists are miniature communities in a sense and like all small communities are prey to extreme mood swings. A feature of mailing lists is the Flame War.

10.6 Spam

Spamming is the practice, famously exploited by Canter and Siegal, a pair of American lawyers, of sending identical messages to every address you can get your hands on. This is usually tried in an attempt to sell some product or service and is likely to get you banned from every group you contact. You will inevitably receive junk mail as a result of others' spamming, with contents ranging from pyramid selling schemes to Web page registration services. Please do not indulge in this practice.

If you genuinely wish to advertise a Web site through a mailing list, write and ask the administrators for permission. If the Web site is of interest to their subscribers, they will usually say yes.

10.7 Threads

A thread is a subtopic, which takes on a life of its own within a mailing list or newsgroup. Like Flame Wars, threads thrive inexplicably and die just as suddenly. (See also Chapter 11.)

10.8 Flames

Flames are irate messages sent to a user before the sender has taken time to think! On a mailing list, a single flame can often start a vicious and unprincipled exchange, inciting more and more people to air their opinions in a thoughtless and provocative fashion. Greatly amusing to the innocent bystander, they are a waste of bandwidth and often result in network administrators closing mailing lists down.

As a rule of thumb, if you find yourself typing a furious response to a list posting, try and exercise some restraint – if it escalates the war, then there is no useful outcome.

10.8.1 Flame avoidance

It is impossible to avoid upsetting somebody, sometime. However, it is possible to avoid most of the more irritating habits that might cause people to flame you.

The following is a form that has been circulating the Internet for some time. The original author is unknown, and this particular version is edited from a message sent to the Leeds-United Mailing List in May 1998. It is not intended to be used seriously, rather to remind people that there is a way of behaving and a way of misbehaving – this form points to the many ways that you can inadvertently trample over the etiquette of the Internet.

```
*************************************************************
Dear:
You are being gently flamed because.
_____

GENERAL
_____

[ ] you SCREAMED! (used all caps)
[ ] you posted the inanely stupid 'Make Money Fast' article
[ ] you posted the inanely stupid '$250 Cookie Recipe' article
[ ] you posted an inanely stupid magic weight-loss article
[ ] you posted an inanely stupid cheap s**t at high prices article
[ ] you posted an inanely stupid 'Fix Your Credit' article
[ ] you posted an inanely stupid 'Good Time Virus' warning
[ ] you repeatedly have shown lack of humor
[ ] you have a SIG with more than 4 lines of ASCII graphics
```

[ ] you assumed that AOL/CIS/Prodigy founded the Internet
[ ] you assumed that the Internet is a US only phenomenon
[ ] you repeatedly requested info on where to find XXX stuff
[ ] you repeatedly harassed people with androgynous names like Chris,
    Jamie, or Rajhatmalhaban, with 'Are you a girl?' or 'M/F?' questions.

FOR LISTERVS (Open discussion Groups)

[ ] you sent a please remove me from the list message to the list
    rather than the list-server
[ ] you continued a boring useless stupid thread
[ ] you repeatedly posted to the same thread that you just posted to
[ ] you repeatedly initiated incoherent, flaky and mindless threads
[ ] you posted a piece riddled with profanities
[ ] you advocated Net censorship
[ ] you repeatedly assumed unwarranted moral or intellectual superiority
[ ] you are under the misapprehension that this group is your preserve
[ ] you are apparently under compulsion to post to every thread
[ ] you are posting an anonymous attack
[ ] you responded to an obvious troll
[ ] you posted an obvious troll
[ ] you neglected to do research on the chosen subject
[ ] you asked a question that was covered in the available FAQ
[ ] you redundantly covered the same point over and over
[ ] you crossposted excessively
[ ] you used long lines, i.e. you didn't break up your lines after 60-
    70 characters, thereby making it hard to quote your post
[ ] you posted a request to send business/get well cards to a little
    boy with cancer who is trying to break the guinness book record
[ ] over 90% of your post was quoted from a previous post
[ ] you considered the following to be reliable reference sources;
        [ ] Golden Books' 'Exploring Science', printed 1955
        [ ] Ripley's Believe it or Not [ ] News of the World
        [ ] The National Enquirer [ ] The Sun   [ ] NY Post
        [ ] The Beano   [ ] Pravda   [ ] OMNI Magazine
        [ ] Company Marketing Hype   [ ] The Simpsons
        [ ] An unidentified, but obviously stupid, person or publication

In the future, you may wish to;
[ ] not delete the 'welcome to the list' message you received when
    you joined
[ ] allow boring and useless threads to die
[ ] remember that not all newsreaders are threaded
[ ] recall that there are academic and commercial users on the net
[ ] remember that the Internet is multinational
[ ] consider that others may know more about certain subjects than you
[ ] exercise some humility
[ ] be careful of where you are crossposting to
[ ] 'lurk' without posting for a few days to learn the forum of a
    group
[ ] get used to being mocked
[ ] stop volunteering for Armed Forces pharmaceutical experiments

I would like to suggest that, for the common good, you;
[ ] wait at least two hours before responding to another post
[ ] read the FAQ (frequently asked questions) list for the group
[ ] learn to use the 'kill' command to eliminate erroneous posts
[ ] selectively respond to threads after reading all new messages in
    that thread
[ ] voluntarily apologise in a brief post
[ ] no longer contribute to this mailing list
[ ] no longer contribute to any mailing list
[ ] no longer contribute to the gene pool
[ ] look into the possibility of medication for the above problems
[ ] familiarise yourself with the history of the Internet
[ ] familiarise yourself with the concept of:
        [ ] patience   [ ] tolerance   [ ] caution
        [ ] common courtesy   [ ] succinctness
        [ ] vocabulary   [ ] higher brain functions
        [ ] Other:
[ ] Reinstall whatever failed mental operating system you are
    currently running on

Please save this message and review it occasionally to determine your
progress towards being;
[ ] a useful member of Internet society

[ ] a less annoying member of Internet society
[ ] a human being
[ ] a fully-functional human being
[ ] a tolerable poster
[ ] integrated into humanity
[ ] reintegrated into the wild
[ ] Other:
****

10.9 Summary

After reading this chapter, you should understand enough about how e-mail works to be able to send and receive messages with and without attachments. You should be able to easily track down a mailing list covering a particular topic, and you will be able to find more detailed information on encoding standards than is supplied here.

10.10 Exercises

1 Send an e-mail to yourself, containing the message 'Just Testing' with a subject line of 'Test Mail'.

2 Send an e-mail to yourself with a binary attachment consisting of an assignment paper.

3 Check your mail folder to see if these messages have arrived yet.

4 Detach the attachment and make sure it is still readable by humans.

5 Locate, using the resources listed in this chapter, a mailing list concerned with

   a) an academic topic that interests you

   b) a hobby (music, sport etc.).

6 Subscribe to both these groups

7 Check your mail folder to see if you have received confirmation of subscribing.

8 Carefully save the instructions telling you how to unsubscribe.

9 Unsubscribe from one or both lists.

11 USENET NEWS

11.1 Aims of this chapter

After reading this chapter you should be able to describe Usenet news and explain the mechanisms upon which it is based. You should appreciate the difference between a newsgroup and a mailing list. You should know how to use a news client, how to find suitable newsgroups for your requirements and how to subscribe to them and unsubscribe from them. The subject of newsgroup etiquette is also dealt with and you should be aware of some simple strategies for staying out of trouble.

11.2 What is a newsgroup?

In order to understand what a newsgroup is, it is necessary first to understand Usenet news itself. If a mailing list is compared to a party, or a bar, Usenet news amplifies the effect as though every party and bar were connected to every other party in the world. Conversations in one party would be accessible from another.

Before the World Wide Web, Usenet news was practically synonymous with the Internet. Usenet is not the Internet, but it is a genuine worldwide distributed discussion system. It consists of a set of 'newsgroups' (approximately 14,000 at the time of writing), with names that are classified hierarchically by subject. 'Articles' or 'messages' are 'posted' to these newsgroups by people on computers equipped with a news client. These articles are then broadcast to other interconnected computer systems via a wide variety of networks.

Like a mailing list, Usenet news works via a client–server arrangement. News messages are delivered to a news server on your university network or at your ISP and relayed from there to the client on your computer. News is updated by the Newsfeeds on the network backbone comparing and updating their contents regularly, each server being in touch with several others – thus maintaining currency even when parts of the network are down. Most news servers will keep messages for about seven days – the sheer bulk of traffic (approximately 400 mb per day) makes it impractical to store messages for any longer.

JANET, the educational network that provides news to universities and colleges in the UK, has six Newsfeeds, each one being fed by one or more different ISPs. The news is then propagated to local servers all over the country.

The scale of Usenet news is difficult to comprehend in any meaningful terms. In 1994 users were estimated to send 40 million characters a day into the system, the equivalent of 1,000 copies of this book. Given the phenomenal rate of growth of the Internet, double this figure would not be unreasonable today. Based on these figures, the unavoidable conclusion is that any message sent to a Usenet newsgroup may be read by tens of thousands of people!

Thankfully, unlike mailing lists, Usenet news does not send you all the articles as e-mail. Instead, you use a news client to access the news server and download only the headers of the messages, which are arranged into threads – self-contained conversations within the group. This allows the user to select the messages that look interesting and download those alone.

The kind of people that use Usenet news are many – business people, academics, computer programmers, conspiracy theorists to name but four categories. Basically all of human life is here including the Good, the Bad and the Ugly – the principle of censorship is alien to the Internet community, however JANET and certain ISPs have taken steps to exclude groups whose content is likely to break local laws.

11.3 What news client should I use?

Predictably, both Microsoft Explorer and Netscape Navigator include news clients with the browser. However both have elected to bundle the news client with the e-mail client which is possibly a little confusing to the new user as news and e-mail provide very different functions. There are selections of stand-alone news clients available from the usual FTP sites (Tucows, Jumbo etc.), which offer more sophisticated yet easy to use features such as thread monitoring, offline reading and multi-tasking.

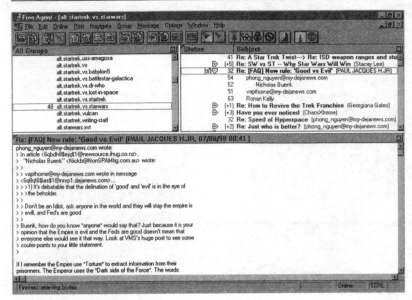

Figure 11.1 Free Agent

The best free news reader for Windows, without doubt, is **Free Agent**, available from Forté at

http://www.forteinc.com/

For the Macintosh platform, **Newswatcher**, available from

http://www.tss.no/%7Elink/NewsWatcher/mt/

is probably the best free news reader available.

Figure 11.1 shows the interface for Free Agent. There are three windows which the user can adjust by dragging and dropping the borders. The windows represent a hierarchy of detail – beginning at the top left, the view contains all the available newsgroups. Clicking on the newsgroup of choice causes a dialogue box to appear asking if you want to view all or a sample of the available message headers in that group. These appear in the window at top right. Clicking on a message header causes the message to be retrieved and displayed in the window at the bottom of the screen.

You can also see, in the message header display, that messages are arranged in threads – each message tagged with an addition sign can be expanded to reveal the messages spawned by this thread.

One of the best features of Free Agent is economy. If you are connected to the Internet by modem, you don't want to stay connected for any longer than possible. Free Agent allows the user to mark message headers for downloading, by right clicking on the message header and choosing the appropriate option from the menu. The next time you connect to your ISP, choose **Get Marked Message Bodies** from the **OnLine** menu to download the messages you have chosen to read.

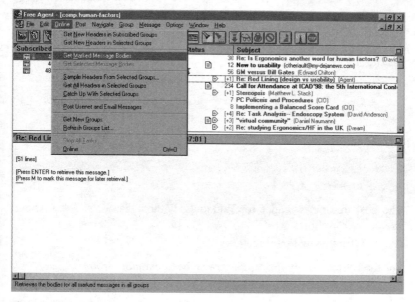

Figure 11.2 Downloading selected messages with Free Agent

Configuring a news client is simple – all it needs to know is your e-mail address, the address of your news server and your SMTP server for outgoing mail. Your news server is almost certain to be called **news.someCollege.edu** or **news.someCollege.ac.uk** for those studying in the UK. If this does not work, check with your Computer Support. Similarly, your SMTP server is likely to be called **post.someCollege.edu** or **mail.someCollege.edu**. The dialogue for configuration can be found in the **Options** menu on all news clients.

The News client supplied in Netscape Communicator, behaves slightly differently in that it has a shared interface with the e-mail client. To access the news facility, choose **Subscribe to Discussion Groups** from the **File**

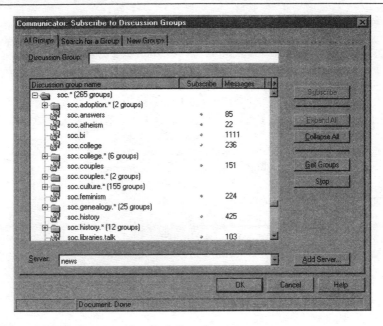

Figure 11.3 Netscape News dialogue

menu. The dialogue box in Figure 11.3, allows you to enter the details of your news server, and select newsgroups to subscribe to. After this has been done, the news server and the discussion groups subscribed to will appear as folders below your e-mail folders in the Inbox pull down menu. While this innovation has its good points – it supports subscription to multiple news servers, all messages appear in the same place – it also hides the difference between the mediums, the understanding of which is critical if you are to get the best out of either e-mail or Usenet news.

E-mail between two people is like a private conversation and can be used in a variety of different ways reflecting the relationship between two people, just like the telephone. Mailing lists encourage people of similar interests to communicate on a one-to-many basis. This may often lead to a private conversation 'off-list' between two members, but generally conversation reflects the focal point of the list. Usenet news is a giant step beyond either of these, messages are read by thousands of people in the popular newsgroups – your audience could be compared in size to that of a local radio host, except that it would not be restricted by geography.

Communication on such a large scale is certainly affected by the differences in culture, language and tolerance that are inevitable in a global society. This tends to mean that the most successful users of the medium write very focused pieces, using short, clear sentences for the sake of being understood.

11.4 How do I find the right newsgroup?

There are over 14,000 newsgroups to choose from; however, since they are arranged in hierarchies it is not difficult to locate the ones that are of interest. The top level of the hierarchy includes dozens of sections, but there are six sections large enough to be described as main:

alt	Alternative groups
comp	Computer related groups
misc	Groups that don't fit easily into other categories
rec	Recreational activities
sci	Scientific groups
soc	Social and cultural issues

Each one of these sections is subdivided:

alt	9,397 subgroups
comp	912 subgroups
misc	135 subgroups
rec	708 subgroups
sci	206 subgroups
soc	265 subgroups

This narrows the field substantially and you will find that many of these sub groups are further divided: **soc.culture** contains 155 groups, each one devoted to a specific cultural group, for example:

soc.culture.europe
soc.culture.french
soc.culture.esperanto
soc.culture.filipino
soc.culture.indian

Some of these may be divided further, for example, **soc.culture.indian** is divided into eight further groups:

soc.culture.indian.delhi

soc.culture.indian.gujarati

soc.culture.indian.info

soc.culture.indian.jammu-ka

soc.culture.indian.karnataka

soc.culture.indian.kerala

soc.culture.indian.marathi

soc.culture.indian.telugu

11.5 Subscribing to a newsgroup

Joining a newsgroup is a matter of finding one which you think will be interesting, and choosing (in Free Agent) subscribe from the **Groups** menu. Once a group is subscribed to, it will appear automatically in the groups window, giving you the option to download all new messages. Clicking on the title bar of the window in Free Agent, shown in Figure 11.4, allows the user to toggle between Subscribed Groups, All Groups and New Groups.

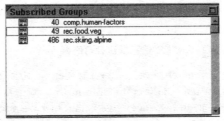

Figure 11.4 Free Agent – Groups window

Unsubscribing from a group is done by right-clicking the group and choosing 'delete'. One thing to bear in mind with Usenet news is that the thousands of articles you may be tempted to download all take up space on your hard drive, so purge the groups periodically. Free Agent always prompts you to choose to save messages (or not). Unless you really have a good reason to save them, for example research, don't bother – there will be plenty more messages tomorrow!

In Netscape, subscribing to a group is done through the dialogue shown in Figure 11.3 – simply highlight the group and click on the **Subscribe** button. Selecting this group from your Inbox will automatically cause Netscape to retrieve the headers for that group.

When subscribing to a newsgroup, be sure to check if an FAQ is available, before you dive in.

11.6 FAQs

A FAQ is a Frequently Asked Question. The answers to FAQs are often updated regularly in the group, as a list. Even if an FAQ is not listed in the headers you see when you subscribe, the chances are that one will exist. A good place to look for the FAQ for any newsgroup is the FAQs by Newsgroup list maintained by Oxford University Libraries Automation Service, at

http://www.lib.ox.ac.uk/search/search_faqs.html

This Web site contains the FAQs arranged hierarchically by newsgroup, also by category.

There are two reasons for checking the FAQs. The first is that you might find the answer to your question in the FAQ, and secondly, it will give you a quick look at the base from which the group is working. You may find that the level of conversation is too technical or too basic for your needs.

11.7 Newsgroup etiquette

We have already discussed, in Chapter 10, section 10.4, e-mail etiquette, and that discussion is equally applicable in this context. The difference between mailing lists and Usenet news is that there is a far greater risk of upsetting people in the larger forum – this is simply a matter of probability. Many Usenet users have only a vague interest in the group they are sampling and many people hold beliefs that are both strange and rigid – so brace yourself for the unexpected flame.

That is not to say that Usenet news is practised in a lawless and aggressive atmosphere reminiscent of the Wild West, it only seems that way if you are a strongly opinionated individual with a forthright style! In fact many groups on Usenet are conducted in a very professional atmosphere and are extremely useful.

These are some Usenet specific rules that may keep you out of trouble:

Keep your postings on topic – there are more irritating things than messages asking 'does anyone know where the bee keeping newsgroup is?' on

comp.lang.java, but it is hard to know what they might be!

Do not cross post excessively – cross posting describes the practice of sending messages to every newsgroup you can think of – the borderline between cross posting and spamming is very thin. This will cause offence because most users subscribe to many groups in the general area of their interests. Cross posting ensures that your article or question will crop up in all of these groups, whereas one or two may have been more appropriate.

Do not post your first year course work problems to newsgroups. In the context of science based groups, your course work problems will seem trivial to the professional readers out there and you are likely to suffer extreme flaming as a result. You are also likely to get found out as most lecturers also subscribe to the newsgroups concerning their subjects and interests.

Remember that your audience may not have English as a first language, so try to keep it short and simple.

When replying to a posting, check the thread to see if anyone else has made the same observation – repeating their posting is a waste of bandwidth and people who have to pay for their access are not likely to relish spending the extra connection time downloading superfluous messages.

If, after scrupulously observing all these rules, you have a problem with someone persistently flaming you for no obvious reason, take the debate off group. E-mail them explaining your position in reasonable terms – try not to let the situation escalate. There are few things more amusing (for others) in Usenet news than watching a flame war from a safe distance. If the abuse continues despite your best efforts, bin their messages before reading them or as a last resort, write to the postmaster at their mail domain, enclosing a copy of the offensive mail and complain.

11.8 Searching Usenet news

Deja News at

> **http://www.dejanews.com/**

is the only Usenet specific search engine available. Other search engines will return results from Usenet news, but Deja News is designed for the purpose and allows the user to search archives dating back several years.

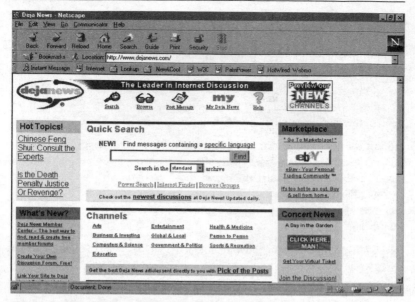

Figure 11.5 Deja News Usenet search engine

Deja News also allows the user to search for newsgroups, using a directory-like mechanism called channels. The user chooses a channel from the list and upon entering the channel, can use the search facility immediately, or drill deeper into the channel by choosing a subcategory from the 'Browse by Topic' menu. Ultimately this will lead to a list of newsgroups touching on a particular topic. In the tests I ran, returns using this method were surprisingly poor – computer programming and software for example returned only four groups. A more effective way of using the resource is to use the power search to look for specific terms.

Searching for a term in Deja News is done in the same way as for ordinary search engines – simply enter the term into the 'Quick Search' box, bounded by quote marks and press 'Go!'. Alternatively, the 'Power Search' facility allows the user to specify a range of groups (e.g. alt.*), a date range (From and To boxes supplied), Author and Topic.

11.9 Summary

Usenet news is very different from Listserv mailing groups and carries its own etiquette to be observed in addition to the normal rules of e-mail. There are thousands of newsgroups arranged hierarchically, the contents of which are propagated from server to server around the world – it is said to take approximately 72 hours for a single message to appear on every server in the world. Usenet news is both a resource for researchers and a recreational pastime. Details of forthcoming academic conferences can be found in the appropriate groups as can details of planned invasions from outer space. Not everything you read on Usenet news is true.

11.10 Exercises

1 Use Deja News to find a suitable newsgroup to subscribe to.
2 Check for the existence of an FAQ on the newsgroup. If there is one, read it!
3 Subscribe to this newsgroup and lurk – read the postings that look interesting, for a few days. Observe how long it takes for a simple question to be answered and monitor the thread to see if anyone comes up with a better answer than the first one.
4 If, after a couple of days, noone has duplicated or bettered your intended answer, post it to the newsgroup.

12 | THE CUTTING EDGE

12.1 Aims of this chapter

This section provide pointers to resources for content providers, that is, people who want to create Web sites. There are thousands of pages on the Web devoted to content provision, this chapter points to the resources that have proved to be both accurate and useful over a period of time.

12.2 W3C
http://www.w3.org/

The World Wide Web Committee, or W3C, is the body which recommends standards which software manufacturers such as Microsoft and Netscape are expected to adopt. The original ideas behind the Internet depended on maintaining an open system which anyone can access. This idea can only be successful if standards are adhered to.

The development of HTML as a language has happened with great speed as commercial interests became aware of the vast potential in the Web. Many enhancements have been implemented independently of the W3C by Netscape and Microsoft, the two main players in the game. Of these enhancements, the successful ones such as Frames have been adopted by the W3C in a recommended standard. Unsuccessful ones such as the <BLINK> tag which causes text to flash on and off in an eye-catching and irritating fashion have not been adopted. In the space of five years, HTML has moved from being a primitive mark-up tool designed to mark up documents for display over a variety of media, to a fairly sophisticated language which relies on a combination of technologies to give multimedia facilities to a network based Web browser. HTML v4.0, aims to restore and enforce many of the original aims in that it firmly separates content from presentation and places emphasis on the Document Object Model for the delivery of multimedia to the desktop.

Presentation, in the form of rules affecting the visual formatting of document elements is now the responsibility of style sheets, which may be embedded in an HTML file or imported from the server. The advantage of this is simply that it is possible to define in a single file, a 'house' style which once defined may be applied to any number of documents.

The Document Object Model states that documents are made up of objects which may be manipulated by scripts or programs. There are, broadly, two types of object – external objects defined outside the document, and internal objects defined inside the document.

External objects include Java Applets, Images and Movies. Internal objects include Pages, the HEAD and BODY of a page, Paragraphs contained in the body, arranged in a hierarchy. By manipulating these objects it is possible to bring a much greater degree of control to bear on the interface, than would be possible with plain HTML. For example, we could define an online test which would reveal the answers after the test had been completed, images could be made to move around the page etc. Much of this development has been done by Microsoft and Netscape, and the implementations in their browsers are still different in certain ways, but it is thanks in no small part to the efforts of the W3C that we have a situation where documents can be displayed similarly on both browsers.

The Web site contains the specifications for all HTML standards, plus news of various ongoing projects which may be of interest.

12.3 Web development: general

The Web Developers Virtual Library
http://www.wdvl.com/

This is an excellent and informative site, containing tutorials, links and advice on all aspects of Internet development. It is particularly strong on CGI programming and Perl.

Developer.com – Tutorials
http://www.developer.com/classroom/tutorials/

This site is the ultimate programmer's dream, containing links to tutorials on every aspect of Web programming including Active Server Pages, ActiveX, CGI, HTML/DHTML, Java, JavaScript, Perl, Push Channels, VRML and XML.

12.4 Java

Java is the programming language that made programming fashionable. It was responsible initially for bringing animation and interaction to previously drab Web pages, but has now repositioned itself as the language of choice for most serious network application development.

The Java API
http://java.sun.com/products/jdk/1.1/docs/api/packages.html

This is the gateway to versions 1.1x of the Java Application Programming Interface. It contains a complete list of packages, classes and details the inheritance chain, the return and argument types for all methods. An invaluable resource.

The Java Tutorial
http://java.sun.com/docs/books/tutorial/index.html

The definitive online tutorial, this is updated as the language is updated and for those who find the API too dry, provides an invaluable resource.

Dick Baldwin's Java Programming Tutorials
http://www.phrantic.com/scoop/onjava.html

According to students, and who better to judge, this is the best set of tutorials on the Web, unfussy and easy to follow. There is a tutorial here for everyone.

12.5 Perl

The Practical Extraction and Report Language was, until the arrival of Java, the only way that interactivity through forms could be implemented on a Web site. The actual mechanism which allows this interaction is CGI, the Common Gateway Interface which allows a Web server to retrieve information from a form and pass it to a program for processing. Perl is the dominant language for CGI based interactivity and is likely to remain prominent for a considerable length of time. It has established a loyal following, largely due to the comparative simplicity of its use and the quirky way in which it has been promoted by its inventor, Larry Wall.

Perl Tutorial
http://www.catt.ncsu.edu/projects/perl/

A very good Perl Tutorial, written by Scott Sams.

12.6 JavaScript

JavaScript, was for some time, a language in search of a use. It has finally found its niche as the major component of Dynamic HTML. JavaScript is an object based scripting language, sporting a Java like syntax and a closely integrated relationship with the Web browser. It is usually embedded in an HTML page, but may be called from a separate file, stored on the server. Using JavaScript constructively it is possible to perform a variety of operations on a page and on the browser itself. For example, enforce form validation, by checking for empty fields when the user presses the submit button, and generate HTML pages dynamically in response to user actions.

JavaScript API Reference
http://developer.netscape.com/support/faqs/jsref/

The developers' reference, for the Netscape version of JavaScript.

Voodoo's Introduction to JavaScript
http://www.webconn.com/java/javascript/intro/

Very well written introduction to the language. This tutorial makes a difficult language seem easy. No mean feat!

The JavaScript Source
http://javascript.internet.com/

For those who can't be bothered to write their own, the JavaScript Source is an excellent resource with hundreds of 'cut & paste' examples.

12.7 XML

XML or eXtensible Markup Language is, like HTML, a subset of SGML. Unlike HTML, the programmer can make up their own tags and in doing so define a document style describing the data contained in the document. HTML describes the structure of a document, in terms of its objects. XML gives us the opportunity to describe the structure of the data itself. This book might be marked up as an XML document in terms of its chapter structure, each chapter containing an Aims, several sections and a conclusion. This makes XML documents even easier to catalogue and search than HTML documents. It is widely believed that XML will become the language of choice for Web sites demanding any kind of searching or re-ordering facilities.

XML, Java and the future of the Web
http://sunsite.unc.edu/pub/sun-info/standards/xml/why/xmlapps.htm

Discussion of XML, giving valuable insight into its positioning in the WWW.

XML.Com
http://www.xml.com/xml/pub

Excellent collection of XML related resources, articles etc.

Microsoft XML Home
http://www.microsoft.com/xml/default.asp

Very good resource with links to some extremely impressive examples.

BYTE Magazine
http://www.byte.com/art/9803/sec5/sec5.htm

Weaving a better Web, *Byte* magazine's excellent commentary on the state of the art today. Comparisons between Netscape and Microsoft's implementation of various Web related technologies.

12.8 DHTML

Dynamic HTML is the name given to a confluence of three technologies, JavaScript, HTML 4.0 and the Document Object Model. The combination of these technologies allows the author to implement sophisticated interactive elements in Web pages, such as animations occurring in response to mouse movement, areas of text revealed or hidden, even changes to the format of a page.

Dynamic HTML in Netscape
http://developer.netscape.com/docs/manuals/communicator/dynhtml/index.htm

The definitive reference for the Netscape implementation of DHTML.

12.9 Linux

Linux is the operating system most likely to cause ripples in Microsoft's pond. It is a Unix clone, designed to work on x86 Intel processor based architectures. This means PCs! It is smaller and faster than Windows, and better still, it is free. There are commercial releases such as Red Hat, SUSE and Caldera, but none of them are expensive, the fee covers the documentation. The source code is distributed with the system and this is what is causing the really big problems for commerce.

Linux is a part of the Free Software movement whose credo is that software should be free, not necessarily in terms of money, but in the sense that source code should be available so that people will modify it and make their modification public. Linux has evolved in precisely this fashion, having been contributed to by thousands of programmers worldwide. Incredibly, it has moved from being a computer geek's playground into a respected operating system which is making inroads into the commercial world. Corporate interests such as Netscape are now releasing products designed for the Linux platform. Perhaps its most notable success is as a host to Apache, the Web server that delivers more Web sites to the desktop than any other product. Apache, too, is free!

Linux Online
http://www.linux.org/index.html

Linux UK
http://www.linuxuk.co.uk/

The Linux Documentation Project
http://sunsite.unc.edu/LDP/

The Linux Resources
http://www.linuxresources.com/

12.10 Summary

This chapter has covered the technologies that will carry the Web into the future. If you want to get involved in Web programming at any level, whether it be as a designer or as a Web guru, this chapter should provide some useful pointers. The importance of the W3C in this area cannot be overstated, without Tim Berners-Lee, in all probability, the Web would have become another proprietary program and we would be paying heavily for the privilege of using it. Instead, Microsoft, the world's largest and most powerful software company have been forced into releasing one of the most popular software packages in the world, free!

GLOSSARY

Anonymous FTP Public FTP servers allow users to log in using the word anonymous as a user name and their e-mail address as a password.

Apache Probably the most widely used Web server software on the Internet. It is free, reliable and easy to administer.

Archie An Internet service that retrieves the FTP locations of named files.

ASCII The standard numerical representation of characters; 128 decimal numbers represent a set of letters, numbers and punctuation marks. Extended ASCII character sets have a further 128 numbers representing foreign characters, mathematical symbols etc.

Bandwidth Literally, a measure of the range of frequencies required to transmit a signal. The wider the bandwidth, the more information can be transmitted.

BBS Bulletin Board System. Small specialised groups allowing downloads and messaging.

CGI Common Gateway Interface. Until recently, CGI was the only way in which http clients could interact with applications on a remote server. Typically used to retrieve results from a form on a Web page, process them and return a result to the remote browser as a Web page.

Command Line Command Line interfaces are mainly Unix or VMS based. Programs are run by typing a command in at a prompt; e.g. $ Mail (starts mail package in Unix).

Compuserve American Internet provider notable for their business oriented forums and the enormous number of free CD-Roms given away with Computer magazines offering one month's free trial.

Cyberspace The word coined by William Gibson in his seminal novel *Neuromancer* to describe an electronic alternative universe. Commonly used nowadays to refer to the Internet.

Database Databases hold information. Many Web sites are electronically linked to large databases, e.g. Catalogues.

Dial up Connection Internet access can be gained from a PC, using a modem to dial in to an Internet Service Provider, over a standard telephone line.

Directory A hierarchically organized system of file storage used by computer operating systems.

DNS Domain Name System. The system used to assign human readable addresses to computers.

DOS Disk Operating System. MSDOS (Microsoft DOS) is the basis of Windows 98.

E-mail Electronic mail.

FAQ Frequently Asked Question. Newsgroups often have their own FAQs, designed as a resource for new members. This saves identical questions from being posted daily. Always read the FAQs.

File Information is stored electronically in files. A group of files may make up a computer program, a binary file may store a picture or a program, an ASCII file may be used to store text.

Flame An abusive e-mail message posted to a newsgroup or individual.

FTP File Transfer Protocol. Used to download files from the Internet and to upload files to a server, e.g. Web pages.

GIF Graphics Interchange Format. One of the commonly used formats for images on the WWW. Used mainly for icons (due to the reduced number of colours it supports) and animations.

GNU The Free Software Foundation project that provides free software for Unix users.

Gopher Gopher is a text driven interface used to locate information. It involves making choices from a succession of menus until the information is found.

GUI Graphical User Interface, e.g. Windows 98, X Windows, Apple Macintosh System x.

Hacker Someone who gains unauthorized access to computer networks is called a hacker; alternatively used to describe computer programmers.

Home directory On logging in to a computer network, the current directory is called the home directory for each user.

Host A computer attached to a network is sometimes referred to as a host.

HTML HyperText Mark Up Language. Used to define Web pages.

HyperText A system allowing multiple references to documents to be embedded into a document, allowing the user to 'jump' from one document to another. This system underpins the development of the WWW.

IMHO In My Humble Opinion. Abbreviation used in e-mail messages.

Internet Wide Area Network consisting of many networks joined together by the use of TCP/IP protocols.

Internet Address Every computer connected to the Internet has an Internet address, consisting of four numbers between 0 and 255 separated by dots. For example, 127.0.0.1 is the default address used to describe 'this' computer when a computer is acting as both client and server.

IRC Internet Relay Chat. A system allowing users using a text based interface to converse with one another over the Internet.

ISP Internet Service Provider.

JANET Joint Academic Network used to interconnect universities and colleges in the UK.

Java Programming language becoming increasingly widely used to implement distributed applications on the Internet. Also used to provide interactive programs on Web pages.

JavaScript Scripting language used to provide client side processing on Web pages.

JPEG Joint Photographic Experts Group. A graphic file type, using a different compression algorithm to GIF. Usually used for large pictures as the compression ratio is better than that for GIF.

LAN Local Area Network. The smallest self-contained networks.

Linux A free, Unix derived operating system used to convert Intel based architectures to Unix work stations. Much loved by computing students for its complexity and high administration overhead. Installing Linux on an old 486 PC is an excellent way to prolong the useful life of the computer, and to learn by experience, the ways of Unix administration.

Listserv Mailing list administration program.

Log In To identify yourself to a computer or network, you must provide your user name and password. This process is known as logging on.

Majordomo Mailing list administration program.

Modem Piece of hardware used to transfer digital data into analogue data suitable for transferring over the telephone network. A modem at the other end of the link converts the data back into its original format. Modems may be external or internal to the computer.

MUD Multi User Dungeon. Computer mediated role playing games are extremely popular on the Internet. A MUD provides a forum for the players of particular games.

Netiquette Internet version of etiquette, describing the acceptable way to behave on the Internet.

Packet The format in which information is transmitted along cables.

Phreaker A hacker specializing in accessing telephone networks.

Ping Unix originated program used to test a connection over a network to a specific host. The command Ping (Internet Address). Sends a packet to that address and reports back the time taken for a reply to be received from that address.

Protocol A set of rules establishing the communication between two computers.

RFC Request For Comments. A series of documents detailing Internet standards.

Search Engine A WWW resource allowing the user to search the Web, using phrases as a search term. Searching is usually not discriminatory, typically returning many thousands of pages if the search term is common.

Server A program capable of recognizing and reacting to requests from a client, e.g. a Web server, a mail server. Often a dedicated machine is used to house a server.

SGML Standard Generalized Mark up Language. The basis of HTML and XML.

Shareware Much software available over the Internet is termed shareware. The idea behind shareware is that users can try it before they buy it. Increasingly sophisticated methods are being used to prevent people from trying it indefinitely.

Smiley Juxtaposition of punctuation marks, used to convey emotion said to resemble a face, such as ;-}

SMTP Simple Mail Transfer Protocol. Used to send e-mail.

Snail mail Derisory term used to describe the post office delivery system.

TCP/IP 'Family' of protocols upon which Internet communication is based. TCP is Transmission Control Protocol governing process to process communication; IP is Internet Protocol, governing host to host communication.

Telnet A protocol allowing the user to log in to a computer remotely and to operate the remote computer from the local keyboard.

Time Out Processes often have a time out period assigned, to prevent hanging the system. This might be used for example to stop trying to connect to a remote host if no reply is received within 30 seconds.

Unix An operating system much loved by computer scientists, upon which the Internet was developed.

Usenet news Internet news network arranged in a number of hierarchies, e.g. alt, comp, rec (Alternative, Computing, Recreational). Users may subscribe to a newsgroup and interact with it by reading the messages and sending replies (contributing to a thread) or by posting original information/ questions.

UU-Encoding A method of converting binary files into a format suitable for transmission by e-mail.

Virus A potentially harmful program which is carried from computer to computer in an executable file. The most common virus found in education is called FORM, resident in the boot sector of disks.

VMS A command line based operating system still common in education, where VAX computers are used.

WWW The World Wide Web, or as modem users sometimes refer to it, the world wide wait. The graphical parts of the Internet.

WAIS Wide Area Information Server. Allows users to browse various information sources.

White Pages Internet directory listing users.

Windows 98 The de facto standard for multimedia PCs. Most new computers come Internet-ready with Windows 98 installed. A TCP/IP stack is provided including FTP, Ping and Telnet programs plus the Microsoft Internet Explorer Web browser.

XML Extensible Mark Up Language. New language, widely tipped to revolutionise the way information is processed on the Internet. Allows the development of tags that can be used to identify information by type. This readily allows the assembling of meta-information describing the contents of a set of documents.

INDEX